The Soul of
the White Ant

EUGÈNE N. MARAIS

The Soul of the White Ant

With a biographical note by his son.

Translated from Afrikaans by Winifred de Kok.

THE SOUL OF THE WHITE ANT

by Eugène N. Marais

First published in Afrikaans under the title
Die Siel van die Mier

Originally published in 1937.

This edition copyright ©2009 Osiran Books

ISBN 978-0-9802976-5-2

OSIRAN BOOKS

web osiran.com

email info@osiran.com

CONTENTS

ORIGINAL PUBLISHER'S NOTE

EUGÈNE MARAIS was born in a farming community near Pretoria in 1872. Journalism was his first career, but he later studied law in London, and by 1910 was in Johannesburg trying to establish himself as an advocate. Increasing depression finally drove him to retreat to Waterberg, a mountain area in northern Transvaal.

Settling near a large group of chacma baboons, he became the first man to conduct a prolonged study of primates in the wild. It was this period that produced *My Friends the Baboons* and provided the major inspiration for *The Soul of the Ape*.

He returned to Pretoria to practise law, to resume his career as a journalist, to continue his animal studies and to write poetry in Afrikaans.

In 1926, the year after he had published a definitive article on his original research and conclusions about the white ant, a world-famous European author took half Marais's life-work and published it as his own. This plagiarism may well have been a major factor in Marais's final collapse.

Plagued for many years by ill-health and an addiction to morphine, he took his own life in March 1936.

ORIGINAL TRANSLATOR'S PREFACE

THE NAME OF EUGÈNE N. MARAIS is known to all Afrikaans-speaking South Africans as a writer of short stories and verse. He himself, however, would wish to be remembered for his lifelong study of termites and apes. He began his working life after leaving college as a journalist, then studied medicine for four years, but eventually took up law.

A scholar and a man of culture, he chose nevertheless to live for a period extending over many years in a 'rondhavel' or hut in the lonely Waterberg mountains, learning to know and make friends with a troop of wild baboons, whose behaviour he wished to study. He tamed them to such a degree that he could move among them and handle them without any fear or danger to himself. At the same time, he also examined the other end of the chain, and studied termite life. This was a study which often meant tremendous hard work and needed endless patience.

During those years, Eugène Marais was not concerned with any sort of publicity. However, a friend persuaded him to write an article for the Afrikaans periodical *Die Huisgenoot*. This proved so popular that the author was besieged with requests for more research information. The articles continued for almost two years.

His years of unceasing work on the *veld* led Eugène Marais to formulate his theory that the individual nest of the termites is similar in every respect to the organism of an animal. He observed that the workers and soldiers resemble red and white blood corpuscles, while gardens with fungus are the digestive organ. The queen functions as the brain, and the sexual flight is similar in every aspect to the escape of spermatozoa and ova.

About six years after these articles appeared, Maurice Maeterlinck published his book *The Life of the White Ant*, in which he described the organic unity of the termitary and compared it with the human body. This theory created great interest at the time and was generally accepted as an original one formulated by Maeterlinck. The fact that an unknown South African observer had developed the theory after many years of extensive labour was not generally known in Europe.

Excerpts from Marais's articles had, however, appeared in both the Belgian and the French press at the time of their publication in South Africa. Indeed, the original Afrikaans articles would have been intelligible to any Fleming, for Afrikaans and Flemish are very similar.

No one who reads this book, based on the articles published so many years earlier than Maeterlinck's book, would hesitate to give its author the honour due to him.

Eugène Marais intended writing a fuller and more scientific volume, but this intention was frustrated by his untimely death.

– *Winifred de Kok (London, 1937)*

EUGÈNE N. MARAIS

A biographical note by his son

EUGÈNE NIELEN MARAIS was born on January 9, 1872 in Pretoria. He was the son of Jan Christian Nielen Marais of Stellenbosch, who traced his descent to a Charles Marais, a French Huguenot. Into this family had married Baron van Rheede van Oudtshoorn, who had been sent out to be Governor of the Cape but had died on board ship in Table Bay, and Dr. Nielen, an American doctor who had come out to South Africa.

Eugène Marais received his first definite schooling in English from an Archdeacon Roberts in Pretoria in whose school he won a 'prize for divinity' because he could recite the whole of the Catechism of the Church of England. After a journey by ox-wagon through the bushveld he was taken to Boshof in the Orange Free State, where he again went to an English school and later to the Paarl.

At the end of the 1880's he was back in Pretoria, and in a few years seemed definitely to have adopted journalism as his profession. At first he was a parliamentary reporter of the Volksraad, but because of his caustic comments on the proceedings he had the distinction of being expressly excluded from the press gallery by a resolution of the Volksraad.

He became Editor of various papers, both English and Dutch, and his whole-hearted support of General Joubert against Kruger resulted in his being tried for high treason, on which charge he was acquitted by the Supreme Court in Pretoria. During this period of his residence in Pretoria he showed great interest in animals and insects, and was never without tame apes, snakes, scorpions, and the like.

In 1894 he married Miss L. Beyers in Natal, but she died the following year. The loss of his wife had a profound effect on him, and accentuated the sombre side of his nature which had already occasionally clouded an otherwise bright-spirited temperament.

In 1895 he left Europe with the intention of studying medicine, but he was persuaded by friends in the Transvaal to take up law. He made the change, much to his subsequent regret, and at the Inner Temple in London qualified as an advocate. He studied medicine at the same time, however, and only the Boer War prevented him from qualifying. He was on parole in England during the Boer War until the opportunity presented itself of going on an expedition to Central Africa, from where he intended to take medical supplies and explosives which he had collected to the Boer Forces across the Limpopo.

While still in Central Africa, where he contracted a severe case of malaria, he learned of the conclusion of peace in 1902. The stores and supplies were buried, and he returned to Pretoria via Delagoa Bay. During his travels he had added greatly to his store of knowledge of the habits of insects and animals.

In Pretoria he began to practise as an advocate, and produced a book on Deeds Office practice. He was still interested in his newspaper *Land and Volk*, for which he wrote in what was considered 'Afrikaans'. His poem *Winter Nag* heralded the new Afrikaans movement.

In 1910 Marais went to Johannesburg, where he again practised as an advocate, but his distaste for the work, coupled with increasing depression, made him give up his practice and move to the Waterberg district.

There, he made an intensive study of birds and beasts. There was no natural phenomenon which escaped his eager mind. He wrote an article for the Government Agricultural Journal on the drying up of Waterberg which was reproduced by the Smithsonian Institute in their annual report. At the same time he was contributing articles on snake poison and stories to the Afrikaans press.

In the district he freely gave of his medical knowledge to help the poverty-stricken population, and acted for years as Justice of the Peace.

But by the end of 1915 his health was so bad that he had to have careful attention, and he was taken to Pretoria, with the happy result that after some months he was able to resume his practice as an advocate. He had chambers nearby and was a close friend of the late Mr. Tielman Roos.

There was again a period of literary activity, but constantly failing health made him give up his practice. There followed a period of practice as an attorney at Bronkhorstspruit and Heidelberg in the Transvaal.

By this time he had completed the draft of what he hoped would be his chief work, *The Soul of the Ape* – a study of the behaviour of apes and baboons and the comparison of their mental processes, as far as these could be gauged, with those of man.

His delight now was to use the newly-fledged Afrikaans as a medium of expression, and the opening it offered for the introduction of new words and modes of expression was eagerly seized by him. While poems, stories and articles flowed from his pen for newspapers and magazines in Afrikaans, he also contributed to English scientific journals in English.

In 1928 another breakdown in health brought him to Pretoria, where he kept up his journalistic work and endeavoured to give form to his work on the termites and ants. There is much that he would have added and possibly much that he would have corrected in this present work, had his health permitted him to give undivided attention to the work. But it was not to be, and on March 29, 1936, he committed suicide on a farm near Pretoria.

Of a singularly pleasant nature, he was adored by and adored children, and especially in his later years could almost always be found in their company.

He has a clear and assured niche among the most noted writers in Afrikaans, and his scientific work and theories written in English have received special notice in America and Europe.

THE SOUL OF THE WHITE ANT

1

The Beginning of a Termitary

SOME YEARS AGO, an article about 'white ants', as termites are commonly but incorrectly called, appeared in a South African journal. Almost everything that naturalists tell us about these insects is important and interesting, and Dr Hesse's article was exceptionally so. The article also made another fact clear; how very little has been done in our country to study the behaviour of animals. Nevertheless, a lot of research has already been done and is still being done in other countries. Everything that Dr Hesse told us was the result of long and patient observation in America and Europe. None of his facts, however, were relevant to our South African termites.

The life-history of most of our South African ants and termites is in every way just as wonderful and interesting as anything that has been discovered in South America. Over a period of ten years, I studied the habits of termites in an investigation into animal psychology. Such observation reveals new wonders every day. To mention one instance, the functioning of the community or group psyche of the termitary is just as wonderful and mysterious as that of people. It has however, a very different kind of psyche, similar to telepathy or other functions of the human mind which border on the supernatural.

When writing about all these wonders, there is a bewildering array of material available. It is, in fact, hard to know where to begin.

I want to tell you about the most common of our termites or 'white ants'. I am also going to explain how anyone may observe what I have. Indeed, readers may even discover new wonders for themselves. Most of these facts have not been published before, nor even discovered by scientists.

The common termite, which is so destructive to wood of all kinds, and builds 'ant hills' or termitaries on the open *veld* (or bush), is known throughout South Africa. I will tell you a little about the beginning of its community life.

The beginning of a termitary dates from the moment when the termites fly, after rain and usually at dusk, in order to escape their numerous enemies. Even here, we see a remarkable instance of the wonder of instinct. The termites, beginning their thrilling flight, know nothing about enemies. They have never been outside the nest before. The peril of their existence is to them a closed book. Yet nine times out of ten, they don't fly until the birds are safely in their nests.

These flying termites are at least twenty times as big as the others of the nest. They are also quite different in colour and form. A termitary must be seen as a single animal, whose organs have not yet been fused together as in a human being. Some of the termites form the mouth and digestive system, while others take the place of weapons of defence, like claws or horns. In addition, others form the generative organs. These flying termites are the generative organs of the colony. Every one of these winged insects is a potential king or queen. The four beautiful wings have taken months to develop and grow to perfection. Months elapse – or even years in very dry districts – before an opportunity for flight occurs. They will never fly until there has been rain, and the reason is obvious. After the flight, they must seek immediate shelter in the ground. When the ground is hard and dry, this is impossible.

It is interesting to follow the flight of the termites carefully from the moment they emerge from the nest. They crawl out of a little opening, thousand upon thousand. There is obviously much excitement in the termitary. Sometimes the flyers are escorted to the opening by workers and soldiers. The first impulse of the flying insect as it emerges is to try its wings. It flutters and tries to lift itself into the air. If it fails, it climbs a grass stalk and takes off from this height. It is very important to fly though, even if it is only for a few inches. Both flying and protection from its enemies are essential features of this stage of the termite's life.

The object of the flight seems to be to spread the insects over as large an area as possible, just as some plants spread their seed. Some of the termites rise high into the air and travel for miles before they settle. Others sink to the ground, only a step or two from the old nest. No matter what, it is essential that they learn to fly, as it is the sole purpose of their existence.

I will describe one of the ants which has flown and settled in the grass nearby. It is impossible to tell the two sexes apart. However, let us take an example and assume it is a female. The first thing she does is to discard her wings. She does this with a lightning-fast movement; it is so fast that we cannot follow it with the eye. One moment we see her with her wings intact, the next moment she steps away, and her four wings are lying on the grass.

It took months for her wings to grow. For years perhaps, she has lived in subterranean darkness, preparing for this one moment. For a period of three seconds, for a distance of perhaps three yards, she enjoyed the exquisite thrill of flight and with that, the object of a great preparation has been fufilled, and the fairy-like wings are flung aside like a worn-out garment. So her wings are discarded straight away, and she walks about rapidly for a few seconds.

You become aware that she is seeking a suitable place for some further purpose. You are not aware what the purpose

Soldier and worker termites

Winged adult termites

Female termites after shedding their wings

is, and her immediate behaviour does not clear things up for you. You must watch patiently if you want to find out what she intends to do. When she has found a suitable spot, she does something very strange. She comes to rest on her fore-feet and lifts three-quarters of the hind part of her body into the air. She remains stationary in this position, as still as if she were merely the statue of a termite. If you become impatient and walk away, the secret of the flying termite will remain a secret to you forever. What is she doing? She is busy sending a wireless SOS into the air. It is important to stay patient a little longer. There are only a few people who have seen this miracle.

What does the signal consist of? I *think* I know, but I doubt if you will guess what it is. It is only possible to find the clue if you have studied the signals of insects. You may of course think of some sound which cannot be heard by the human ear. You may know of the little South African *toktokkie* beetle (a beetle of the genus *Psammodes*), that knocks in similar circumstances. However, the termite's signal is not a sound. One can prove that by an experiment. For the moment, the fact is that the signal consists of something far beyond our own senses. Yet the male becomes aware of it over incredible distances! How does this happen? Well, it *does* happen, and the female termite's sexuality means that she will make the first advance to a male.

If you wait long enough, you will see another termite come flying through the air, and you will notice that although his flight appears awkward and almost involuntary, he can steer a course and choose a direction, even against the wind. The male sinks to the ground, sometimes a yard or two from the place where the female is standing motionless in her curious posture. As soon as he lands, he makes the same lightning-fast movement which we have already seen in the female, and there on the ground, his wings also lie. His haste is terrible and irresistible. Over and through the grass he crawls, so fast that we can barely follow him with our eyes. He is looking for the originator of the signal which he received high up in the air. Within a few minutes, he has found her. The female's body has been motionless all the time. Her body has been raised high in the air. However, the instant the male touches her with his antennae, she is affected by his excitement. She begins to run away as fast as her legs will carry her. The male immediately comes behind her. They are now beginning the final search. They are house-hunting, and the male leaves this reponsibilty to his wife. It must be a good house, for they will live in it for a long time. Soon they have found their new home, and while they are digging the front door, we will leave them for a while.

There are even stranger things connected with this little drama, which the inexperienced observer will not be aware of. I have explained the urge to flight. If those two termites had not flown, none of the events we have watched would have occurred. Instinct is something which only works step-by-step. If you destroy one step or omit it, then the whole system of their community collapses. Nature wishes the 'white ant' to spread. If the nests are too close together it would be bad for the communities. As a result, they receive wings and must fly. However, flight is only one step in their sexual life. If this step is omitted, their sexual life, and their very existence, ends there and then.

For as long as two years, the two sexes may live in the same nest after they have grown wings. They are in constant touch with each other but there is not the least evidence of any sexual life. They *must* crawl out of the nest, they must fly, and must settle and lose their wings. It is only then that their sexual life begins. Once it does, it is immediate. If you prevent them flying and break off the wings, both male and female die. It will be imposible to continue the race.

The length and distance of the flight is of no importance. It may last hours or only a second; it may cover miles or only a few inches. The force which we call 'instinct' means that they

Termite mounds in Litchfield National Park, N.T., Australia.

must pass through every stage. The termites must take every step, or they are doomed. If you take a male and female just as they are emerging from the nest and place them beside each other, even in the closest contact, you notice that they take not the least interest in each other. They struggle to get away from each other. If the female flies a few inches, the whole process is carried out and finished. If the male circles round even once, and then he is forced to land near the female, it is only then that events will take their normal course. A second in time, three inches in space, one flutter of wings – are to the termite a gulf as wide as infinity, dividing two kinds of existence. To us, it may appear only a small dividing line. However, the insect may not overstep it, not even with human assistance.

2
Unsolved Secrets

THERE ARE A LOT OF DETAILS related to the building of the termitary. However, I will focus on behaviour, as it important to understand for purposes of comparison. All behaviour, both animal and human, is of importance to the psychologist. Behaviour *is* psychology – at least it is all of the psyche we know or can study. For purposes of comparison, for comparative psychology – especially if you begin at the top of the ladder with the apes – the field available for study is in fact, not very large.

The task falls to the king and queen of feeding and attending to the first children. After the children are fully grown, they take it upon themselves to undertake all the work of the community. In the meantime, the queen grows larger and fatter by the hour. Her small neat body vanishes in increasing layers of fat. It becomes an unsightly worm-like bag of fat. To make matters worse, her mate, in addition, has the blessing of appearing to having discovered the secret of eternal youth. He remains as attractive, active and young as he was on his wedding flight. The queen, on the other hand, has become an immovable worm. It is very hard to imagine that that she ever fluttered gracefully as a young termite. It is almost conceivable that the male could cast around for a mate as equally attractive as himself. However, it is to his great credit that he does not behave in this way!

His attachment to his queen seems to keep pace with her own growth. If the palace cavity is opened or attacked by a predator, he rushes round in consternation, but always returns to her side. There is no question of saving his own life in flight. He clings to her gigantic body and tries to defend it. If the attack is sufficiently ruthless, the male termite will choose to die at the side of his queen. This is an outstanding example of the enduring commitment and fidelity of termites.

A queen in any kingdom, whether the human or animal world, is often known as 'the mother of her people'. The termite queen quite literally fulfils this role. She is the only mother of the millions which form the community. It is an extraordinary fact that every individual is born from her.

This means that she does not have to take any responsibility for the 'nursery'. All she is expected to do is to keep on laying an endless stream of eggs. This is to counteract the enormous daily loss of workers and soldiers, despite their excellent methods of defence. It is a remarkable feature of termite society that the death of thousands of individuals can be made good by an unending supply.

It is important to note that in actuality, every termitary differs in its growth, but for the purpose of clearly understanding their society, it will be assumed that the environment of our nest has been such that development is entirely normal, and it has not been subject to any disturbing external influences.

The first workers begin to build a palace for the queen. Deep below the surface of the earth, from three to six feet, they prepare a hollow chamber. As years go by, this is gradually increased in size, and the earth which is excavated is taken to the surface, where it is used to form the thick defensive crust. The queen is placed in this hollow chamber. It fits her so well that it would be easy to assume it has been built around her.

In fact, I do not think this actually happens – but at this stage, most of my conclusions are mere guesswork. No human eye has ever seen what actually takes place. No one has ever

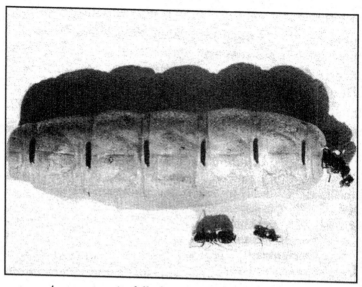
A queen termite full of eggs, with two soldier termites

discovered a way in which to watch the termites at work in the queen's chamber. They work in pitch darkness, and to let light into the chamber is as great a handicap to the termites as the sudden destruction of the sun would be to us, as we cannot see in complete darkness.

The queen continues growing until, compared with the ordinary termite, she reaches a gigantic size, and becomes an immobile, still mass. The only part of her which gives any sign of life is the little head, which remains unchanged. If you dissect the skin and body carefully and examine it under a microscope, you will be convinced that during her later stages of growth, the queen is unable to make any voluntary movement, except of course of the head.

You may think she could move like some worms do, by contraction and expansion. However, you will find that no part of the body behind the head can be controlled by what was once an intricate central nervous system. I also believe that it is not possible for her to regain the power of movement, even temporarily. I have not seen any indication of this, even when emptying the sac for a while. Besides, the very nerves in the body have changed into fluid. The theories that the queen is able to move by contraction and expansion, or that she gains a temporary power of movement, have to be discarded.

An examination of the queen's life history shows that her first palace is a cell made of termite earth. This rapidly becomes as hard as cement. Usually she just neatly fits into it. She is always much too huge to use the door of the cell as entrance or exit. If you wish to remove her, you must break down the cell. The king and the workers, however, can come and go quite easily. She is fed and the eggs which she never ceases laying are removed to the breeding grounds by workers appointed to this task. The king apparently does nothing; he appears to be a mere hanger-on in the palace. Still, the queen goes on growing. Here in her first palace, she has not yet attained even one-third of her eventual size. At last, she very nearly fills all the available space in the cell. There is barely room for the tiny workers to carry the eggs away across the inanimate bulk.

A terrible tragedy appears to be imminent. It reminds us of the question: what will happen if an irresistible force meets an immovable mass? The human observer is not in a position to intervene and avert the threat of this terrible fate. Scientific knowledge should not be instrumental in interfering with the way the termite world is constructed.

But termites have never worried about it at all. They have a solution ready – a very simple one. Just before her majesty finally outgrows her cell, they build a second one, half as big again as the first. It is parallel and adjacent to the first, just as hard, and with a narrow door. The queen is then removed and placed in the second cell. There is space for her to grow here for perhaps another year. So she gets transported from cell to cell, until there have been about six changes, with the queen in the last and biggest. The chamber doors are always equally small, much too small for the queen to come or go by.

There is another fact which makes the whole matter even more complicated. One could easily prove by measurement that the queen's subjects could not possibly move her. The lifting power of one termite can be estimated fairly closely, and the area of the queen's body available for workers to grasp during lifting can be measured. During the later stages, it would need thousands more termites to lift her than there is available space for grasping the body.

So we have the following facts:

- The queen is incapable of movement.
- The doors of the cell are too small for her to come or go by.
- The insects cannot lift her.
- Yet she vanishes from one cell, to appear in another.

The only explanation that seems feasible is that there are several queens and that it is not the same one each time. If the first gets too big for her cell, she is killed and eaten, and the workers carry a potential queen into the second cell where she develops into a queen. This seems to be the most reasonable and simple explanation.

Unfortunately, it is not true. The analogy with bees has led to a false conclusion; we have been deceived by the analogy of the bee world, which makes queens, kills, and moves them.

It is quite an easy matter to mark the termite queen, and so prove that it is the same queen which gets moved. I have tested many theories, but have never found one which coincides with all the facts. Perhaps one day, a future Fabre will discover the truth.

3
Language in the Insect World

SHORTLY AFTER SHE DISCARDS HER WINGS, the flying queen sends a signal into the air. This is always answered by the appearance of a male flying through the air. What exactly the signal is will now be explained in detail. In order to understand the language of animals, one must first of all learn its ABC. It is also necessary to bear in mind that some previous assumptions about human and animal behaviour need to be re-examined and unlearned. We will therefore begin at the very beginning.

An individual member of any animal race which wishes to communicate with another at a distance can use one of three things: colour, scent or sound. If you think of colour, scent and sound simply in terms of the impression which these make on a human being, then it is not feasible to translate this to the termite world.

There is one kind of termite which constantly signals by means of sound. If you have ever slept in a house in which those termites are at work, you will know the sound well. It is a quick *tik-tik-tik*. You can also hear this if you place a microphone through a hole made into a termitary. You will easily observe that not only do the termites make this noise, but that other termites at a distance hear it and immediately react to it by their behaviour.

If you catch one or more of the signallers and examine their anatomy under the microscope, what you find is very interesting. There is not the least sign or suggestion of any kind of auditory organ; not even the most primitive kind of ear. There is not even a single nerve that could possibly be sensitive to what we call sound. We find the same regarding colour and scent. The termites undoubtedly use both colour and scent as a means of signaling, yet there is not any organ that resembles an eye. There is not even the faintest spot of pigment which might serve as a primitive eye. The termites are quite blind, yet sensitive to an indirect ray of light far below the threshold of perception of the human eye. That is, they can become aware of a very diffuse light not shining directly on them, which a human eye could not perceive. This can be proved by experiment. As for any organ of smell, that, too, seems to be completely absent.

An observation of another insect, the little *toktokkie* beetle, will greatly help to explain the secret. If you wish to learn to know the *toktokkie* really well and to learn his language, you must tame him. The beetle will become so used to your presence that he won't alter his behaviour, even when conscious of being observed. He is very easy to tame – at least the gray-bellied one with pale legs, not the rough-backed one. He readily learns to accept being captive and studied.

Most South African children are familiar with the *toktokkie* and have heard him make his knocking sound. The beetles are easily located, as you can often see them on the road or beside it. If he does not get a fright and fall down dead with stiff legs, as dead as the deadest *toktokkie* which ever lived, then you see him knock, and of course hear him, too. He looks round for some hard object, a piece of earth or a stone, and knocks against it with the last segment of his body – three, four, four, three! This is his morse code. He then listens for a moment or two, turning rapidly in many directions. His behaviour is very like that of a human. His whole body becomes an animated question mark. You can almost hear him saying:

"I'm positive I heard her knock! Where can she be? I hear it again!"

He answers with three hard knocks, and then he takes himself off in great haste and runs a yard or two away. He then repeats the signal in order to get a further true direction, and so he continues until at last he arrives at his partner's side.

If you study the behaviour of many *toktokkies* during the mating season, you will occasionally have to follow one for an incredible distance in the direction of the answering signal. He can hear the signal over a distance which makes the sound absolutely imperceptible to the human ear. It is at this stage that his behaviour warrants study by a psychologist. If the beetle is studied closely under the microscope, there is still no sign of an ear, or any other complex or nerve which might be linked to sound and hearing. But in spite of this we still think of the behaviour of the *toktokkie* in terms of sound or hearing!

Our version of a laboratory is a stretch of natural *veld* or a fairly large garden where it is possible to study tame *toktokkies*. The observer will soon discover that the *toktokkie* is one of the most credulous of insects. That is, when he is dominated by sexual desire, he will believe everything you happen to tell him. Knock on a stone with your fingernail in his own morse code – and at once he answers. You can teach him quite easily never to knock except in answer to your signal. You can succeed in doing this by not knocking for several days unless he has become perfectly quiet. After a day or two, he will have learnt to knock only in answer to your signal and will answer immediately.

Now get a small, powerful microphone, a headpiece, and three feet of wire (you will find this indispensable in your association with the insect world). The microphone must be so powerful that you are able to hear the footfall of a fly quite easily.

When your *toktokkie* is tame and well trained, it is then possible to test the acuteness of his perceptions. You will discover that they are unbelievably and supernaturally fine.

To continue the experiement, knock on the stone again with your fingernail and gradually make the sound softer until it is quite beyond your own hearing. The *toktokkie* will still continue to immediately answer the signal. Even if you knock with the soft pulp of the finger rather than the nail, so that there does not seem to be any sound at all, still the *toktokkie* answers! Now, take the microphone and place it on the ground with the earphones over your ears. Next, examine its response by knocking on the receiver with the pulp of your finger – a substantial knock, not merely a tap. With a little practice, you can reduce the sound until at last it is inaudible even through the microphone, but still the *toktokkie* hears it!

The solution to the problem is this; it is not sound as such which the *toktokkie* becomes aware of, and there can be no question of *hearing* it. Sound is only our interpretation of certain vibrations in the atmosphere. (Sound cannot travel through a vacuum – you can prove this by sending a sound through a wire inserted in the cork of a thermos flask. It will be imperceptible, except for a faint noise which escapes through the cork.) It is our ear which interprets the vibrations as sound. Beyond the ear, the universe is soundless. Without an ear – or organ of hearing – there can be no sound. But the vibrations which we call sound have a physical function. It is by the exercise of physical force that the drum of the ear and the hammer and anvil bones of the inner ear are set into vibration. In the same way, you can make grains of sand or a thin gas-flame vibrate to a musical note. However, there is another difficulty. The sudden meeting of the surfaces of two physical bodies can result in vibrations of the ether, which are not by any means sound-waves, and therefore have no effect at all on our ears.

We are getting into deep water now. This is where the

study becomes particularly complex and challenging. It would appear that it is vibrations of this kind – waves in the ether, which the ants and the *toktokkie* make use of.

This theory may in fact sound far-fetched, but this explanation links closely to the language of insects. Listen carefully the next time you hear a 'longbreath locust' (apparently so called because it is *not* a locust and the sound is *not* made by its breath). In order to fully understand their physiology, it is essential not to think of 'sound' or 'hearing'. Rather, you must think of vibrations, waves in the ether – which can be sensed by another such locust at a distance of at least eight miles. It is also important to understand this concept when examining the communication which takes place between the outlying sections of termite nests.

This serves as a summary and insight into sound in the insect world. There are two other methods of communication: scent and colour.

Termites continually make use of scents, some of which we can also perceive with our olfactory organ. In the Northern Transvaal there is a well-known termite known as the 'stinking ant'. This creature emits a foul smell to a distance of three or four yards, which has the peculiar property of causing extreme nausea in most people and also in dogs. Then again, all South Africans will be familiar with the characteristic smell of the common termite. This is caused by the discharge of a gas. It is of the utmost importance in the study of termite language to fully understand what the signal of the queen really consists of. After a long period of study, I have come to the conclusion that it consists of something which would affect our senses as *scent* if it were strong enough.

Things always seem pretty hopeless in the beginning when we are dealing with phenomena which lie far beyond our senses, but 'perseverance pays' must be the motto of the traveller along these dark and unknown pathways.

There is another reason for thinking that the signal may be

thought of as scent. You can easily train a pointer to track down the flying termites after they have lost their wings. He will track down a signalling queen for nearly a hundred yards against the wind; with the males, he finds it difficult even over the distance of a yard. But a still more important proof will take me longer to explain.

The following are all the signals used by the termite:

1) *The communal signal,* which is constantly sent out by the queen, who forms the hub of the nest. This serves to keep the community together and enables every termite to recognize every other member of the community. It is a signal which cannot be perceived by our senses.

2) *The call of the workers and soldiers.* This is perceived by us as sound.

3) *Food messages.* (Beyond our perception.)

These three be will examined more closely later on.

4) Lastly, *the sexual signal of the queen,* which is also beyond the reach of our senses.

Throughout nature, scent and colour are used as sexual signals. If there are no brilliant colours, you can be sure that there will be some scent instead.

Allow me to digress for a moment. We have seen how the flight of the termite is the key to which the door to their sexual life is unlocked. Without flight, there can be *no* sexual life. It is simply not possible. I will give another insight. In mammals, the key to their sexual activity is generally *scent,* which may also be allied to colour. This begins in the plant world. The colour and perfume of flowers is of course, purely a sexual phenomenon. In mammals however, scent still remains as the key to attraction, and therefore survival. It is this which makes sexual life possible.

That is why it is possible to keep large mammals for years in a zoo or a menagerie without their sexual urge being activated. It is interesting to study African kudus in relation to this fact. In the Waterberg, I often had the opportunity to closely observe a wonderful sight. For a week or two every year, the kudu cows become scented or 'on heat'. As soon as this passes, the bulls leave the cows and segregate themselves to graze in small herds. Of course they come in contact with the cows occasionally, but never show the slightest interest.

However, when the cows are in heat again, the scent will travel four or five miles on the wind. Prior to this, the bulls were grazing peacefully. Once they get the scent on the wind, it is as if they have been hit by a thunderbolt. They immediately become restless and they eagerly sniff the wind. The whole herd, which a moment before was grazing so peacefully, responds with deafening bellows. They are then lost in a cloud of dust. The only sound now is the clashing of horns and bellowing of rage. Their sexual life is always preceded by the stimulation of the fighting sense. Without the special scent from the cows, their sexuality would not have been stimulated.

This can be easily proved. Take one of the smaller mammals; the kind dependent on the sense of smell. If its olfactory nerves are destroyed or cut by incision (in some cases nature does this with an ulcer), he will never again be sexually stimulated. This is the case even if a male comes into very close contact with a female, including one in heat. External stimulation, in the form of scent or colour, is always essential to stir their sexual interest. The only animals whose sexual interest can be aroused without this outside stimulation are the higher apes and people. In the instance of the ape and humans, the cultivation of scent and colour is both fascinating and mysterious.

It is very interesting to gain an insight into why some women choose to wear perfume. There is in fact, a subconscious reason. The attraction of wearing perfume is linked to a forgotten instinct from the ancient history of our race. The basis of all perfumes is the sexual secretions of several kinds of cats, of deer, and (the most expensive of all), the essential sexual material secreted by a certain kind of whale. These scents are today artificially produced for the perfume industry. Musk is the universal basis of the scent sex signals in animals. Even in humans, this phenomenon may still be found. Indeed, about one woman in every thousand still secretes musk on occasion. As a result, her skin becomes strongly and exquisitely fragrant. As in the case with many such primitive characteristics, this secretion of musk is found more frequently in the monkeys or apes. Nevertheless, that is the origin of the role of scent in sexual attraction. In the primate world, it still plays a significant role.

Scent may also be regarded as waves in the ether, or space. It is false to assume that perfumes consist of gases or microscopic substances. Perfume itself is not entirely a physical substance. You may scent a large room for ten years with a small piece of musk and yet there will not be any loss in its weight.

This has been a way of illustrating what the signal of the queen really consists of. It has provided an insight into the sexual signal of the termite queen. It is actually a wave circle in the ether which our olfactory nerves would perceive as perfume – that is, if our senses were even aware of it.

4
What is the Psyche?

THAT WHICH IS KNOWN as the psyche or soul is something far beyond the reach of our senses. No one has ever seen or smelt, or heard or tasted or felt the psyche, or even a piece of it.

There are two ways in which we can begin to track down the psyche.

In my own innermost self, I become aware of something which is not a tangible part of my physical body. This awareness of course is limited to a part of my own psyche. That of my brother is just as far beyond my direct reach as is the psyche of the termite. I must accept the existence of other psyches because I am told of them. Introspection is thus one method by which I am able to affirm the existence of the psyche. But this is a separate branch of knowledge which at the moment does not concern us.

Now we come to a question which will prove more interesting to us in regard to our observation of the termite. I will try again to be as sparing as possible in my use of scientific technicalities. But I must enlarge on it, and you must be patient and try to understand it if you wish to grasp all the wonders of a termite nest which will be revealed to you later on.

Remember that most of the important definitions which follow are my own, and made on my own responsibility, for what that may be worth. You will search scientific books in vain for confirmation of what I say. Nevertheless I flatter myself that if you really study nature, not only will you find that all I say is true, but that it is the *only* key with which to unlock many dark secrets in the behaviour of living creatures.

Let us first see what science says. The psyche, so say scientific and very logical people, *is a state of matter*. This was also their first definition of magnetism; you dare not say the psyche is something which causes a certain state of matter, for there is no proof of that. But the analogy with magnetism and later discoveries gives us a certain right to say:

First: "The psyche is something outside the reach of our senses; it causes certain states in matter, which states are within the reach of our senses."

It is of course only through movement that we can become aware of this state. This raises the question: what is a psychological movement? Our whole life is a world of movement. We see dust and leaves blowing about in the wind; we see streams flowing and water plants swaying in it. We hear the wind and feel it; we see a little ant carrying a piece of food to its nest, we see an egg apparently unmoving, but if we have the chance of watching it long enough and carefully enough, we see a continuous movement, which eventually results in a chicken. Which of all these movements are movements of the psyche and which are not? While avoiding a deep analyis of logic and metaphysics, it is still possible to state that only movement which has a definite motive can be a 'psychological movement'.

Secondly: Our own psyche is naturally the criterion which enables us to establish whether there is a motive or not.

Logically, this may not be an entirely satisfactory definition, but for the practical naturalist it is sufficient. Secondly, we learn by experience that such movement occurs only in certain kinds of matter – namely organic; that it mostly originates in the organism itself, and is not dependent on forces outside itself. The key word is *mostly*, because there are many motivations in nature which are really dependent on outside forces and yet are psychological movements.

There is the case of the seed of what we call the 'flute reed'. Like a little powder-puff in shape, the seed floats on the lightest breeze like a tiny plane, but as soon as it arrives over a pond or a marsh, the seed sinks to the ground like a bird settling on the water or damp ground. At first sight, this appears to be a truly psychologically motivated movement coming from within the seed, such as we very seldom find in the plant world.

On closer examination, the explanation is that through friction with the wind, the little powder-puff, before it wrenches itself free from the mother stem, receives a charge of negative electricity. The result is that all the fine hairs of the puff spring apart. As long as the hairs are spread open, the seed floats in the air; but as soon as it comes into contact with water vapour, the electricity is discharged and the puff folds up and slowly sinks to earth. By this means, the plant makes certain not only that its seed shall be spread far, but, what is of greater importance, that every seed will land on damp ground or actually in water. Here you have a number of objectives which the plant achieves by utilizing natural forces outside itself. Nevertheless, all these fall inside our definition as movements *with a motive* and therefore, psychological.

Thirdly: Mostly – but only mostly – the movement originates in the organism itself.

The above definition will suffice for the practical naturalist. He will at times come across some puzzles, as for instance the pretended death of the *toktokkie* or the growth of a crystal; but after reflection he will find our definition still suffices.

A few words more about our classification of these motivated movements in nature, and then we will have finished this dry-as-dust topic and can continue with our termites. That all this has been very necessary, you will see later.

To sum up, these 'motivated movements in nature' have been classified as follows:

1) *Motivated movements in the plant world.*
   These consist of four kinds:
   a) Growth (for instance turning towards the light by plants).
   b) Tropism. Induced by outside influences.
   c) Movements dependent on natural forces outside the organism.
   d) Movements which appear to originate from within the organism, for instance the extension of tendrils towards near objects by certain creepers; this may also be a tropism.

2) *Motivated movements in the lower animal world.*
   The most common and most important are movements which originate in the organism itself. External forces of nature are used, but in a manner differing to that of the plants. The peculiarity of these movements is that they always follow a fixed course; the organism can never modify or change its behaviour; and this fixed behaviour is as much inherited as the organs of the body.

It is therefore possible to conclude that all motivated movements are dependent on what we call *memory*. We call these predetermined inherited motivated movements 'instinct'. This is especially evident in its original form in insects. Throughout the whole lower animal world this is unchanged until you come to the apes and humans. It is only then that you find a vast and striking change in motivated movements, both in quality and in quantity.

It is important to establish the role and relevance of the psychology of instinct. The memory which constitutes this instinct is hereditary, in the same way that the physical organs of the organism are hereditary. The following experiment which I carried out will explain what I mean.

The well-known yellow South African weaver bird – there are many kinds, but any kind may be used for this experiment – plaits a wonderful little nest at the extreme tip of a flexible branch, generally over water. You often see their nests at the end of the thin drooping twigs of the graceful weeping willow, but have you ever taken the trouble of watching to discover how the very first piece of grass is tied to the twig and what kind of knot the little bird uses? The full-grown bird is a seed eater, but the little ones are fed on worms until it is nearly time for them to leave the nest. Remember these two instinctive memories:

1) How to build the nest, and
2) How to feed the fledglings.

I hatched the eggs of the yellow weaver under canaries for four generations. The new birds were forced to lay eggs each time without being able to build their characteristic nest. This is the most difficult part of the experiment, but it can be done. Every time these eggs were hatched under canaries, the young ones were fed on a synthetic diet and were never allowed to see a worm or an insect. Nor did they ever see a piece of grass which might be utilized for building. Then I took this fourth generation and provided them with everything which they would need in their normal environment. Remember now, that for four generations they have not seen a plaited nest or tasted a worm. From personal experience, the bird cannot possibly know what to do. There can be no question of individual memory. I expected at least that there would occur some deviation from normal behaviour, but it was not so. When the time arrived for nesting, the birds began plaiting vigorously. They made more nests than they required. This often happens in nature as a means of protection. The eggs were hatched and the young ones were fed on worms!

This experiment shows what I mean by the inherited memory of instinct.

The second characteristic of this psyche is that the individual is incapable of deviation from a certain fixed way of behaving. In other words, he cannot acquire any individual causal memory. Inherited memories are a key characteristic of all behaviour. Even when death threatens, there is no escape. This remains the case even if escape means behaviour contrary to the inherited memory.

Here are two further examples to support this. The black 'road-maker' ants – real ants this time, not termites – are found in many parts of South Africa. They make footpaths, hundreds of yards long at times, along which they bear all kinds of plant and grass seed to their nest. At a distance, you see two streams of these ants, one apparently white, the other black. The approaching ants each carry a white seed; while the retreating ants don't carry anything. The ant carries the seed in its husk down into the nest. Here the husk is carefully removed. The seed is stored, and the husk is deposited outside the nest in a heap. One kind of 'road-maker' ant is a master of a wonderful natural secret which even scientists have not discovered. It knows how to prevent the germination of seed, even when this is placed in damp ground in the dark. The microscope cannot even discover the least flaw in such seed. However, if you pick some of the same seed and place it in exactly the same spot where the ant places his, it germinates within a few hours. These 'roadmakers' are afraid of water. A flood is their greatest natural enemy. This is because they were originally a desert ant; in other words, they are emigrants, and have not yet learnt how to protect their subterranean nest against long continuous rains.

The fear of this arch-enemy of their race is deeply rooted in them. The only solution they have is flight – as early and as far as possible.

If you dig a little furrow across their path and fill it with water, the ants become very confused. On both sides of the furrow, an excited group will congregate. It takes them a very,

very long time to discover that an easy solution would be to make a detour. Before they think of this, however, a grass stalk may be placed across the waterway to serve as a bridge. You will immediately be able to watch their very peculiar and mysterious behaviour. The ants begin to test the dangerous bridge. One by one, they try the bridge with their forelegs, stretching their bodies across it, while they cling to the bank with their back legs. They feel the bridge with their forelegs and antennae. They then become aware of the water and hastily retreat to tell their fellow ants that the bridge is quite unsafe. This is what happens on the bank which is on the same side as the nest, where the unladen ants congregate. On the other side of the bridge, the side farthest from the nest, the behaviour of the ants is quite different. The ants arrive here, each laden with a grass seed. Generally, the seed is so heavy that the ant's progress is both difficult and hindered. What happens at the bridge? With apparently not the least hesitation, each ant steps on to the straw with its gigantic burden. Sometimes it capsizes, but clings to the bridge with all its legs, and still manages to cross. It always succeeds in bringing its load to safety and hurries home to its nest as though nothing had happened.

This is where their behavior becomes puzzling. The unladen ant is afraid to risk its life on the bridge while the laden ant crosses with a load which makes its passage a hundred times more dangerous. The carrying of the burden cannot possibly lessen its awareness of the water.

Take a square piece of tin covered with earth, and push it under the ants congregated on the nestward side of the bridge. Once they are gathered thickly on the tin, pick it up. With a fine brush, mark as many ants as possible with a small red mark on the hind part of the body, and then shake them on to the ground beyond the bridge. Immediately you will observe thay they all rush off along the path, shortly to return each carrying a grass seed. The ants will then cross the bridge without any hesitation, as if they had been crossing bridges all their lives.

43

After a while, some of the marked ants will return from the nest, having safely deposited the seed. When they come to the bridge they stop, and nothing you can do will give one single ant the courage to cross the bridge. You may continue this process until almost every ant is marked with a red spot. In the end, you will have learnt two things:

First, that you will never teach the ants by their own experience that the bridge can be crossed in safety. Secondly, you will never teach the ants that if the bridge is safe for a heavily laden ant it must be, proportional to the load, so much safer for an unladen ant. They prove this for themselves hundreds of times. If you were to continue this experiment for months, the ants would be able to prove this fact thousands of times. Their behaviour never changes or varies, thus reinforcing your observation of their innate behaviour. The unladen ant will never dare to cross the bridge, but as soon as he returns with his heavy burden, he crosses without hesitation.

Can you guess why the unladen ant refuses to cross and the laden ant does not? If you have investigated the psychology of animals, and therefore, the behaviour of the ants, it shows that their motivation is to obtain food. The behaviour of the unladen ant which leaves the nest is determined by only one instinctive urge – to fetch food. In any case, it is not a very strong urge, for it always operates in opposition to the ever-present and very great urge – *the homing instinct*. This is the strongest of all psychological urges, except the sexual urge. Higher up the scale of animal life, we call this urge "home-sickness", *heimweh*. The ants returning with the seed are drawn by two of the strongest urges:

1) *The homing instinct*, and
2) *Bringing the food to safety*.

It is as if you had tied threads to the ants and were pulling them. The thread pulling the ant away from the nest is very weak. When the ants become aware of danger and become afraid, the thread breaks. But the returning ants are drawn by *two* strong threads, which even fear of death cannot break. It is therefore evident that there is a plausible explanation for the apparent mystery surrounding their behaviour.

It is now possible to understand what is meant when psychologists state that the instinctive psyche cannot deviate from the inherited formula of behaviour, and that no individual can acquire a causal memory – in other words, he cannot learn by his own experience.

I also said that the psyche of inherited memories is a force which cannot be turned aside even by death, if escape means behaviour which conflicts with the race memory. As an example of this, I will describe the case of the springboks on the Springbokvlakte in Waterberg. This *vlakte* or plain is an island of open *veld* in the middle of the Transvaal *bushveld*. The springbok is highly specialized for life on the open plain, in other words all his inherited memory is of open plains. He knows how to escape the perils which threaten him there; he knows which is the best food for him there and how he can find this. In addition, he knows when and how to change his environment. He can see and smell over great distances. On this plain in the 1920s, there were thousands of springboks. They have now been exterminated. Slowly but surely people have populated this area by creating farms, fencing off camps, and destroying the springboks. To the west, the mountains rose and to the north lay the endless bushveld, where they would have been absolutely safe. Death lay on the one hand and safety on the other, but they could not take the step which would have saved them. Thousands of other big game, less specialized in their behaviour, fled into the bush and saved themselves from extinction. It often happened that herds of springbok were chased by hunters into the *bushveld*. They always returned, however – sometimes the very same day – to meet death on the open plain.

There still remain two further kinds of 'soul movements' or

instinctive urges in nature, the classification and peculiarities of which you must know if you hope to understand even a little about the behaviour of the termite.

3) *Group movements.* There are some movements in individuals of a community which are determined by some purpose of benefit to the community. We term this phenomenon the "group psyche or soul". You find it in the termites, ants, baboons, apes, and in all animals which live in groups or are gregarious.

Then lastly:

4) *The psyche of individual memory* – that is the psyche of the primate, man and the apes, baboons and monkeys.

When you live with baboons, you soon see that the difference between the psyche of the lowest baboon and the highest mammal (the dog or otter, for instance), is far greater than the difference between the psyche of the baboon and that of man.

What exactly is the difference? We know that the difference is there, but it requires considerable research to understand what it is.

If you ask scientists what the psychological difference is between a baboon and an otter, nine out of ten will say that the baboon possesses powers of reasoning and intelligence which the otter lacks. It would be just as clear if they said the baboon is a baboon and the otter is an otter. Neither answer takes you very far. Another scientist may say that a baboon can learn new habits more easily than an otter. This provides more of an insight but is not a comprehensive explanation.

It is necessary to carefully examine the issue of race memory. This allows us to see the result of it in nature. An example is a land bird that can fly and is very much the same in every respect as other land birds. Gradually our bird begins finding food on the beach. After millions of years, it learns to catch fish in fairly deep water. As soon as this becomes a fixed habit, natural selection begins to operate. The deeper the bird goes into the water, the more chance it will have of survival if it is equipped for this new life, both physically and psychologically. This process of evolution continues for another million years. The bird lose its wings, which now serve as oars; it loses its feathers, which become down; the legs become adapted for swimming – and at last we have the penguin. By the way, you will see I adhere to Darwin's theories: I never saw very much in those of De Vries.

If we observe the penguin or the otter, despite their differences, several important facts are evident. If any sudden change occurs in their environment, they are completely at sea. An example of the otter in these conditions was during a drought once in the Waterberg. It lasted for four years and when all the streams became stagnant, you would find otters all over the *veld* adjacent to the big waterways. There were still pools of water, but these did not contain any fish or crabs. The otter is nimble, and you can teach it to catch birds and other small land animals in the same way a cat does. Yet the otter cannot teach itself to do this. Hundreds of these wild otters died in the midst of plenty. At this time, I managed to get hold of a pair of newborn otters. One of these I sent to Springbokvlakte, thirty miles from the nearest running water. As he was dug out of the nest shortly after birth, he had never seen a river. A bitch reared him with her own litter. He never saw or was given food other than raw meat, birds and other land animals, and he never saw water, except when it was given to him in a dish to quench his thirst.

At the same time, I took a newborn baboon from the mountains to the plain and reared him with a feeding-bottle. Afterwards he was fed on food which was not his natural diet. No opportunity was given him to him to catch or eat a living insect. When both these animals were three years old, they were taken for the first time to their own natural environments. The otter was taken to Sterk river, its orginal environment, while the baboon was taken to the Dubbele Mountains where his mother had been shot. Both were starved for a short while prior to this. This created a wonderful opportunity to observe the great difference in the behaviour of these two creatures.

On being released, the otter hesitated for just a moment or two, then plunged into the water, and within half an hour had caught a crab and a large carp and devoured them on the rocks.

The baboon, on the contrary, was completely lost. He was in the midst of a source of natural food yet, although starving, he obviously knew nothing of turning over stones and catching the living insects which hide beneath them. There is no doubt he would have died of hunger if he had been left alone. When I turned up a stone for him, he retreated from the wriggling insects, and showed signs of fear and horror. With the greatest difficulty, I succeeded in persuading him to taste a dead scorpion, from which I had removed the sting and the poison gland. At last, he was induced to catch a living one, with the result that he was immediately stung on the finger. He chose, amongst other things, to eat a wild mountain fruit that is deadly poison, and his life had to be saved. Such accidents never happen to wild baboons. They have learnt. Our tame baboon also eventually understood all these things, but he had to learn by painful experience.

We see then that nature has done two things for the baboon: a psyche has been provided which is able to acquire individual causal memories; and secondly, nature has done away with his inherited race memory. The baboon is the transition point in the animal world. He has advanced so far that in about fifty per cent of cases, there is no inherited orientation of the sexual instinct, the instinct which is the strongest inherited instinct of all. In humanity, we find no inherited orientation of this instinct at all. Sexual desire may awaken, but the orientation must be learnt in both sexes. How has this extraordinary change in natural behaviour taken place? In the first place, some great advantage must accumulate for the race as a result of the change.

On the whole, the result of inherited memory is to bind a race to a special environment. The penguin to the sea, the klipspringer to the mountains, the springbok to the plains. The more perfect race memory is, the more strictly confined the organism will be to its environment. This is the result of natural selection. The affirmation or belief that selection and development in nature are striving after some ideal state of perfection is incorrect. In every case of highly specialized animals, a *loss* of physical perfection has occurred. An exchange in terms of natural selection always takes place, but the the result is not perfect. When the penguin exchanged his wings for oars, it did not become more perfect; the long neck of the giraffe is a disadvantage in flight. Nature is not a 'charitable institution'. In fact, the environment is inevitably challenging, if not hostile. If this was not the case, there would be no natural selection. It is clear, too, that the species which is bound too closely to a certain environment is at a great disadvantage. If the environment undergoes a sudden change, such a species is lost. It cannot change to a new environment and individuals cannot acquire new memories to enable them to cope with the changes in their environment.

In Africa, it frequently happens that whole species are exterminated by such changes in nature as droughts, locusts, or the arrival of other unknown enemies. To give a species the great advantage of being able to change its environment suddenly, natural selection must cause a change in the very psyche of the animal in question. No single or even repeated physical change can bring this about by itself. There must be psychological change too. The first and most important step is to wipe out the inherited or race memory. Unless this happens, there can be no change in environment. Not only must the race memory be destroyed, but even the possibility of its being inherited must disappear from the psyche – or the change will be useless. Instead of race memory, a psyche must be developed which enables every individual to acquire his or her own causal memory of their environment. It is this change in the baboons which has given them an advantage. Everyone who is familiar with them will acknowledge that this is the case.

The immediate result of this change was to make the baboon a 'citizen of the world'. It can adapt itself to any environment – that is why we find South African baboons in a variety of surroundings. You find them on the fruitful mountains of the Cape, in the big forests and river valleys of the interior, and in the waterless deserts of the Kalahari. In every environment, the baboon acquired new habits. It learnt to catch suckling lambs and tear them open in order to drink the milk in their bellies – throughout half of South Africa. In the Northern Transvaal, the baboon has not learnt this yet. In one district in Waterberg, the baboon has learnt to place a hard fruit on a rock and break it open with a stone. This is evidence of the first use of an implement. Nowhere else in nature will you find such behaviour, except in the baboons and apes.

From all this investigation, we can derive two clear facts. First, there is a vast psychological gulf between the psyche of the baboon and the psyche of the highest mammal below the race of primates. Secondly, the psyche of humans and the psyche of the baboon are exactly the same in quality. The difference is found to be only in quantity.

In the case of the baboon, we are looking at the stream near its source in the mountains. In the case of the human race, we see the same river just before it disappears into the ocean.

Humanity has gone the furthest in this direction. That is the reason why people have conquered the biggest and driest deserts, the Gobi and the Sahara, the highest mountains, the deepest valleys, the tropics and the frozen Poles – and survived. However, the environment extracts a price in return. As has been shown, there is always an exchange. The baboon and the human race paid a high price for their new type of psyche. This price may be so high, that it is bound, surely but slowly, to bring about their natural extermination.

The old animal psyche of race memory does not actually get destroyed. Instead, it is paralysed by a kind of permanent inhibition. It still remains however, and can be artificially stimulated into functioning. This is the greatest discovery I made during an observation of the wild baboon lasting over three years. The so-called 'subconscious' psyche of humanity is not a creation of natural selection which leads to ideal perfection, but is in fact the old animal psyche in a state of inhibition. That is, the instinctive, natural behaviour has been suppressed or altered. In abnormal circumstances, this is released and leads to serious psychological disorders.

This background has been presented to allow a further investigation of the communal psyche of the termite.

5
Luminosity in the Animal Kingdom

THE ORDINARY USE OF LIGHT by the glow-worm and firefly is well known to South Africans. In the Transvaal, the fireflies create an amazing show. On the slopes of the Highveld, they appear at times in such numbers that the riverbeds stretch into the night like streams of light as far as the eye can see. It is difficult however, to know for certain what the motive of this signal is. Despite long, careful observation, it was impossible to see the purpose, if there was one, of the signal. It almost seems as though the insect purposely hides its motive when it becomes aware of being observed.

In this respect, the firefly reminds me of the pollination of one of our grasses, *aristida*. This pollination is very challenging to observe. I remember how I watched one whole day until after midnight at the side of an unpollinated plant. At night, acetylene mine lamps were lit which cast a circle of light as clear as day for nearly a hundred yards round the plant. I went to sleep for a couple of hours and woke to find that the pollination had taken place while I slept. The pollination takes place when you least expect it, an hour or two before daybreak. I also spent many sleepless nights watching the firefly and was still not able to determine what the motive of the signal could be, except possibly that it is a sexual signal. If there is a doubt, it arises from the fact that the sexes are not dependent only on the light for their sexual life. There are other land creatures which also periodically become luminous.

The most fascinating is the large green centipede which is found in tropical parts of Africa. Perhaps this gigantic centipede causes more fear and horror in people unused to handling such creatures than any other. For some reason – which I do not know – this monster sometimes becomes luminous. It is a rare occurrence and I have only seen it twice. The spectacle is one you will never forget and if you encounter it unexpectedly in the dark, it is quite extraordinary. The centipede is about twelve inches long and while the luminosity lasts, the creature, which is usually so quick, appears to be in a state of cataleptic paralysis. It appears as though all its energy is being used for the generation of the brilliant light. So bright is the illumination that fine print can easily be read in a dark room at a distance of two feet. It is difficult to determine what causes the light. A chemist examined all the organs of one of these luminous centipedes and he could find no trace of any known light-giving element. Under the microscope, the light appeared to come from two luminous patches near the ends of each segment of the body. The light is in continuous movement, an irregular glowing and paling. This expands and contracts in concentric circles, coming from an intense centre of white light. The circles of light are independent of each other. Coincident with the change in intensity, there is a constant, amazing change in the colours of the circles of light. Passing outwards from the white centre, the colours appear in the following order: light-yellow, light-green, emerald-green, dark-green, blue, dark-blue, red, purple and violet. The source of the light lies within the body of the insect and is irradiated through the skin. In the glow-worm, the source of the light appears to be outside the skin.

This is yet another example of the unexplored field of work in connection with the signals of animals. The characteristic of luminosity completes the list of animal signals. Similarly, the firefly too, still has elements of mystery.

What is the motive of the light and what *is* the actual light? These puzzling elements often remain when we study animals which make use of well-known forces of nature.

The South African jellyfish, for example, has as a means of defence a charge of electricity, with which it shocks you if it touches you under the water. The whole of the body of the jelly-fish is filled with water. This forms a perfect conductor without insulation, as it is surrounded by sea-water, which is a far better conductor than the human body. In such conditions, it appears impossible for the creature to generate a charge of electricity, and still more impossible to direct it through human skin. The creature simply *cannot* do it – yet it does!

In the discussion of fireflies and glow-worms, it is important to question one theory. The famous Fabre died under the firm impression that he had discovered the secret of the light. On the skin of the insect, we find a white powder, which looks very much like frost. The insect projects on to this two streams of air, and the light disappears in the absence of oxygen. Fabre therefore concluded that the phenomenon was nothing other than oxidation. He had no further doubts and his statement has been repeated by many writers.

However, if it *is* oxidation, then it is a form of oxidation which is found nowhere else in nature, and which the cleverest chemist could not imitate – as this would require a complete revision of all our beliefs about the properties of oxygen.

Oxidation always generates heat, even if it takes place very slowly, as for instance in the rusting of metal. The heat is then generated so slowly that it is not noticed, but still there is heat. If oxidation takes place rapidly, the generation of heat becomes explosive. When oxidation takes place quickly enough to cause light, there must be a previous and continuous generation of heat. Oxidation without this phenomenon is just as impossible as fire without light or heat. If oxygen is necessary for the firefly's light, that does not prove that the light is due to oxidation, as Fabre claimed. If you take several fireflies and test them with a sensitive thermometer, you will find there is no rise in temperature due to the light. One could prove that to produce a light equal in strength to that of the firefly for one hour, the bodies of more than eighteen hundred fireflies would have to be burnt. I would conclude, based on this evidence, that Fabre's theory is wrong.

There is further information that it is necessary to understand about the qualities of light. Some years ago, a Japanese naturalist discovered that the firefly emits rays which affect a photographic plate through the black covering. These rays must be those which are imperceptible to the human eye. I have been unable to test this myself, or to discover whether our fireflies also emit these rays.

6

The Composite Animal

THE DIVISION 'GROUP SOUL' in our classification of psychological movements is one which the human mind finds most difficult to understand. The further we depart from our own psychological characteristics, the more mystified we become. The true group soul is the opposite extreme to the psyche of the primate, which consists of uninherited, individual causal memory of the environment. A perfect example of the group soul can be observed in our own bodies. The human body is composed of a number of organs, each connected by a visible or invisible thread to the central point, the brain. Each organ is in constant activity and has a separate purpose – at least the purpose *appears* to be separate and independent; but on closer observation, we find that all the organs are really working for a communal purpose. The influence dominating all the organs comes from one central point. In no single organ can we find a real independent purpose. Apart from the composite physical body of a highly developed animal such as humans, there is no better example of the functioning of a group soul than the termitary.

The following information may seem to border on the incredulous. However, all the facts are able to be supported and proved experimentally.

Anyone who carefully observes the termite will ask the question, "Why do they continue working? What is the mainspring of this restless activity?" The termite is certainly a restless insect. Do you know that of equally developed creatures, the termite is the only one which apparently never rests or sleeps? However carefully you observe it, you will never surprise the termite at rest or asleep.

What is the aim of this endless toil and struggle? In other individual animals, the environment has provided such animals with great urges. These are the sexual and parental urge, the urge to defend, and the urge for food and drink. These urges constitute the psyche of the individual and dominate its movements. In the individual termite, there are none of these urges to act as a driving force.

The answers to these questions really form the definition of a true group soul. My investigation can be summarized in the following:

1) *All the movements of the termite are controlled from outside the individual.* The termite possesses no trace of free will, or power of choice. The only quality it possesses is automobility – the power of moving itself. It puts itself into motion, but when this motion will take place or what will be done with it is decided and controlled from without. Circumstances may make the termite's work useless and vain; in cases where the simplest insect, individually controlled, would shrink from its purpose, the termite will carry on. It *must* follow the path along which seems to have been predetermined.

2) *The behaviour of the termite is totally determined from without by external influences* – we may call it a thread, by which he is firmly tied to the queen's cell. This invisible influence streams from the organism of the queen alone. It is a power beyond our senses; it can penetrate all material barriers, even thin steel or iron plates.

3) *Distance lessens the influence*: it has power only between fixed limits.

4) *The death of the queen destroys the influence immediately.* Injuries and wounds sustained by the queen weaken the influence in proportion to the size of the injury.

5) *The termitary is a separate composite animal* at a certain stage of development, and lack of automobility alone differentiates it from other such animals.

6) *The termite has descended from an ordinary flying solitary insect.* The development of specialized groups and their amalgamation is a late occurrence in the race-history of the termite.

7) *The termitary is an example of the method by which highly developed animals such as mammals came into being.*

8) *The body of a mammal, with its many vital organs, can be looked upon as a community with specialized individuals grouped into organs,* the whole community forming the composite animal. The higher the development of the animal, the higher the specialization of the groups.

9) *This phenomenon of specialized groups of individuals being developed into different organs and becoming a composite animal can actually be observed today.*

The group soul, which is surely the most amazing psychological phenomenon in the natural world, is the result of this communal life. It gives the strongest proof that it may be possible for a psychological influence to have an effect on an

A group of termites in which can be seen soldiers, workers and nymphs.

organism at a distance. It is important therefore, that we should observe the composite organism and try to understand it. The particular kind of termite on which I based these observations is one of the most common in South Africa, and everyone will be able to study it.

If you make a breach in any termite's nest on the *veld*, it will in all likelihood be the nest of the kind of termite described here. In the break, you will see two kinds of insects. They differ so greatly from each other that without a knowledge of termites, it is virtually impossible to tell that they had the same mother and father.

One is an ordinary whitish insect with strong jaws, and two black spots which appear to be eyes. The other, under a magnifying glass, looks like a nightmarish monster. It is reddish-yellow in colour, but when many are massed together, the red colour becomes dominant. The body ends in a massive triangular head, tapering to a long, black horn-like needle or syringe. Below the neck, there are four almost rudimentary legs, in addition to the other ordinary functioning legs. This needle or syringe is in direct communication with a large reservoir of fluid. In your wildest imagination, you could not create a creature more bizarre. Except for its two antennae, there is no trace or sign of any organ of sense. How and what the creature eats is baffling. The only possible food would have to be a thin fluid. The ordinary food which is carried into the nest must have undergone a great change in the bodies of the other termites before this horned beast could make use of it.

With a fairly powerful magnifying glass, it possible to see at once that the behaviour of these two kinds of termites in the break in the nest is not identical. The syringe-bearers gather in increasing numbers and, with their syringes pointing outwards, quickly form a ring round the opening. If you tease one of these termites with a stiff bristle, it makes a stabbing movement with its weapon in all directions. Eventually, a crystal clear drop of sticky fluid appears at the end of the syringe. This fluid contains

Termitary material.
The photograph below is approximately actual size.

a certain amount of stinging acid. There can be no doubt that these syringe-bearers are there to defend the nest against the enemy, relying on their terrifying appearance as well as their weapons. Apart from this, they do nothing. Protected by this cordon of defenders, the other termites begin working busily. They begin to mend the breach in the nest. From the depths of the termitary, each appears carrying a tiny grain of sand or earth in its jaws. With the help of similar rudimentary legs as those described in the syringe-bearers, the grain is turned about rapidly. Under the microscope, it can be seen that the object of this is to coat it with a similar sticky fluid. It is then fastened to a section of the break in the wall. It cannot fall. If you touch the newly built section, your fingers become sticky, as if you had touched some syrup. This fluid has the property of evaporating very rapidly, and as soon as evaporation has taken place, the stickiness disappears.

One of my theses is that the termitary is a separate and perfect animal, which lacks only the power of moving from place to place. The following explanation will make clear the beginning and development of the group soul. What happens in a wounded termitary has now been established. It is also important to examine a far more developed composite organism before again looking at the termitary.

*

The human body is a machine, and consists of millions of cells, through which blood constantly flows. The fluid consists chiefly of two separate kinds of organism; red and white corpuscles, each of which is a living cell having a life or soul of its own, as well as a group soul. These corpuscles build up the body, mend wounds and attack germs. Metchnikoff's conclusions in this connection, although doubtful in certain respects, are nevertheless generally true.

The attacking microbes are themselves attacked and devoured in the wound or in the natural orifices, or, if they succeed in entering, the fight is carried on in the cells and passages. Every wound swarms with defending white corpuscles. If a germ of disease enters the system, there is an increase of white corpuscles.

Both growth and healing always take place from within to the outside. Covering the vital organs, we have the epidermis or skin, a tough impenetrable covering which shuts out light and air. The corpuscles of the blood are afraid of air and light. The growth of the body is more wonderful and mysterious than may at first be realized. We are far too prone to consider every ordinary natural phenomenon as a kind of established truth, which needs no explanation, like, for instance, the fall of an apple to the ground.

Consider for a moment the growth of the body, with particular reference to the skin. Growth always takes place from within to outward.

However, we do not find a piece of skin being removed, a piece of an organ being built, and then a new skin being grown over the wound. The growth takes place *under* the skin. You would be justified in expecting either that the skin should stretch or that a new piece of the body should be grown on top of the old skin and then a new skin over that, so that if you cut into the body you would find layers of old skin.

Neither of these things happen.

Well, you say, of course the skin grows in the same way that the internal parts grow. It is easy to say this, but we cannot find any proof of it. We know that all growth is caused by the corpuscles in the bloodstream. But we also know that these corpuscles never come into contact with the dermis, or outer skin. How this outer skin grows at the same rate as the other organs we cannot explain. You know, too, that your body consists of several large organs, each of which functions independently. According to our classification, each of these is a separate animal with a separate psyche. Then you have another organ which is the home of the group soul; the brain

– the centre of the community which is the body.

You have learnt by this time that soul and life are identical. Every definition for *soul* will be equally as good for *life*, and vice versa. I have never observed any instance to prove that soul and life are two separate entities. They are one and the same. The only difference lies in the two names, which have, in fact, been given to the same thing.

A small injury to the central point, the brain, is sufficient to cause the immediate death of the whole body. The growth and life of the body can continue only with the help of the red and white corpuscles of the blood. Food is taken through a foramen, the mouth, and, after being changed or digested by certain organs, is absorbed by the corpuscles. Ninety per cent of this food is carried to different parts of the body and used as cells to make new muscle, sinews and bone. A portion of the food consists of unassimilable material. It is important to be aware that this must be absorbed by the corpuscles with that which is assimilable, as this in turn forms part of the assimilable material. Within their own bodies, the corpuscles separate the assimilable and unassimilable, and the waste is eventually cast from the body as excreta.

It has been stated that a small injury of the brain is sufficient to cause the death of the body. Let us now study some of the many peculiar and mysterious aspects of the condition we call 'death'.

We know that a living person can remain in water for ten days without any part of their skin dissolving. The channel swimmers stay in the sea for twenty-four hours, and their skin is quite undamaged by this immersion. Water cannot wash away any part of the living skin, in fact the skin of a living person is as insoluble in water as a piece of rubber. The whole body of a living person is full of elasticity and possesses a great power of resistance to blows from blunt objects. It is necessary to keep in mind these two characteristics:

1) The insolubility of the skin.
2) The general touch-resisting powers and the elasticity of the whole living body.

The change which takes place in these two respects after death is astounding. Have you ever seen a drowned person who has been in the water for some hours? You will remember the gruesome change. What has caused this? As soon as life ends, the epidermis becomes more and more soluble in water. The body immediately begins to lose its elasticity and power of resistance, until at last even a child could poke a blunt object right through the body. To put it plainly, every part becomes spongy and falls into decay. The physiologist expresses all this differently, generally in long Latin or Greek words, but the meaning remains unchanged. He says that as soon as death has taken place, the more complex components break up into simpler ones. Microbes appear to hasten the process. This however, does not help us to understand things more clearly, for the following reasons:

The body consists largely of dead matter. All the cell walls and the outer skin are made up of ordinary dead matter – or chemical substances. What do the corpuscles do to prevent the solubility of the skin and to protect the elasticity and structure of the body? No one knows. The presence or absence of the corpuscles makes this difference vast. A certain mysterious phenomenon in chemistry means that the mere presence of one element can change the chemical make-up of another element.

The same kind of function is played by the living corpuscles in the bloodstream. This secret, inexplicable influence, which their mere presence has on the chemical and physical character of dead matter, is the mystery of life. In the simplest living cell, such as the blood corpuscle, we find something which not only enables it to move, but which also prevents the breaking up of the cell material.

Antagonistic forces of nature are always present, ready to break up the cell. Here we find the beginning of the struggle for life – the attempt to frustrate the hostile forces of nature. The first purpose or urge is a tug of war between life – or the soul – and matter.

This influence, at a distance, of certain substances specially secreted by the body for this purpose, is a well-known biological phenomenon. The human body possesses a number of ductless glands whose function it is to produce certain secretions. The mere presence of these secretions exercises a great influence on the whole physical make-up. The adrenal glands, for instance, produce adrenaline, which is responsible, amongst other things, for the blood pressure. The gland itself is completely isolated from the rest of the body and yet has this influence at a distance.

*

This insight into physiology and biology allows us to apply this knowledge to study the termitary. You may wonder how I can call a heap of dead earth like the termitary a 'living animal'. The termitary is actually no more dead than the dead matter of cell walls which constitutes nine tenths of your own body. We are ourselves no more than dead termitaries, through which circulates a living substance.

If you dissect a termitary, you find, firstly, a tough resistant skin all around it. Under this skin, you find that the whole termitary consists of cells, through which a living stream of termites constantly circulates. As you go deeper, you find large passages, and eventually a hollow. This is partly or entirely filled with more cells, which are of a different consistency from those of the actual heap. These cells no longer consist of earth and are covered, both within and without, with a kind of mould. This mould is often used in South Africa to make yeast.

If you go deeply enough, and observe carefully, you will

find, at the very bottom, a passage which goes right into the earth. If the termitary is an old one and placed on top of a dry *kopje* or hill, this passage descends to an incredible depth. It is the canal by which the termites get their water supply. They continue the shaft until at last they reach permanently moist ground.

On the farm *Rietfontein* in Waterberg, I had the opportunity to follow such a passage to a depth of more than 57 feet through earth as hard as the rock in the side of a mine pit.

Termites need a great deal of moisture. More than ninety per cent of their tiny bodies consists of water, and the whole termitary is always damp and filled with water vapour. Where they manage to get all this moisture in our dry districts would have remained a dark secret, if someone had not discovered the existence of their deep vertical aqueducts.

7
Somatic Death

IN AN EARLIER CHAPTER, some of the effects on the human body of somatic death were discussed.

The final result may be expressed as follows: the chemical constituents of the cell walls or organic material are very unstable. In ordinary circumstances, they tend to break down into simpler elements, or else new and more stable combinations take place. The final result is that organic matter, as such, disappears. Living, moving matter in the vicinity of the cell walls maintains these unstable elements. The final result is that organic matter, as such, tends to disappear. The presence of these living elements safeguards the skin against this ever-present tendency towards dissolution. This is the primary function of what we call *life* or *soul*.

A superficial examination will reveal straight away whether a termitary is alive or dead. In general, the process of dissolution corresponds in function to the dissolution which takes place in the human body. We find exactly the same appearance of undisguised lifelessness. That is, there is a change in smell, although not the same actual odour. This change may be attributed to the same causes; namely, the dissolution of chemical constituents. Accordingly, there is the same immediate loss of the defensive toughness of the skin. The innermost cell structure falls to pieces; only dust and ashes remain.

The similarity of the two phenomena becomes even more

convincing if you examine the termitary in detail.

Firstly, examine the skin. The covering layer of an old termitary, in dry seasons, is thick and impenetrable, as hard as cement. After long periods of rain, it becomes softer, in the same way that human skin becomes softer after long immersion in water. The living stream of termites constantly circulating through the termitary never comes into contact with the outer skin. The termites never renew the skin from the outside. Sometimes, though, you see patches of renewal. The growth or healing, as the case may be, always occurs from within to outwards, just as in the human skin.

The construction of new patches is a peculiar phenomenon, with a particular purpose. As far as the skin is concerned, in an old full-grown termitary, you will never observe the termites doing anything to keep it in condition. Such an old termitary is exposed, year after year, to torrents of rain, terrible droughts, scorching heat, frost, hail and wind. Through all these diverse climactic conditions, the skin remains undamaged.

In cases of actual trauma, through hail for instance, repair takes place by the functioning of the two little creatures in the bloodstream; that is, the two kinds of termite. The living skin in general appears to be insoluble in water. Even during continuous rain, you will not find the least portion of it washing away.

There are occasionally exceptions to every rule. For instance, we sometimes find various forms of abnormal growth, real diseases, which expose the whole structure to danger. The termites are in these cases just as 'stupid' as the bloodstream in a human can be. Sometimes the reason is obvious. You can encourage abnormal growth artificially by stimulation and other influences, both in the human and in the termitary. A common abnormality is the growth of a long, narrow tower which is constantly destroyed by wind and bad weather. This is an abnormal deviation from the usual pointed summit which is found on termitaries amongst trees. The base of the tower is often so small that it is impossible for it to carry the superstructure. Yet every time the tower falls over, it is built up anew. This is not only a great waste of energy, but the abnormality often becomes a danger to the whole community.

This raises a number of additional questions about the complexities of the termite community. What constitutes the difference in quality between the skin of a dead termitary and that of a living one? What keeps the outer layer whole and healthy as long as the living stream continues moving within? What causes the cell walls to retain their structure intact, and what causes them to fall apart as soon as the termites die? There appears to be only one theory which conforms to modern scientific knowledge: there must be some kind of power projected from the living stream which influences the chemical constituents of organic bodies. This functions in the termitary in the same way as the human body.

It is extremely important to understand that the termitary must be looked upon, not as a heap of dead earth, but as a separate entity at a certain stage of development. It is essential to grasp this, as it provides further insight into this perfect example of a group soul and its characteristics.

To reiterate, these are the similarities between the human body and the termitary:

1) We have just seen that both possess some mysterious power which exercises an influence on the whole structure, and is the cause of its stability.

2) Both the human body and the termitary consist of a structure of cells covered with a thick skin. An inhabitant of Mars who had learnt enough of our Earth to divide matter into organic and inorganic would not hesitate for one moment to classify a piece of termitary as organic. The only

difference would be that for a piece of human body, a microscope would be required to study the structure, whereas in a termitary, it could be viewed with the naked eye.

3) Moving through the cell structure under the skin, we find a living stream consisting of two kinds of organisms. In both humans and the termite, they have the same functions. The white blood corpuscles quickly form a defensive circle round a wound. They are there for apparently one purpose only, to prevent the invasion of strange, hostile organisms. The other, or red, blood corpuscles busy themselves with repairing the injury. From the innermost part of the body, these latter bear material for new cells, which are eventually covered with new skin.

   If you make a wound in the skin of a termitary, the living stream is seen at once. The red syringe bearers form a circle of defence around the wound. Their only function is to prevent the entry of enemies through their frightening appearance, or by actual defence. For purposes of defence, they secrete a clear, sticky, stinging acid. The other termites of the living stream at once begin repairing the wound. They carry material from the depths of the termitary to build up the new cell structure. This is eventually covered with new skin.

4) The human body takes food through a foramen – the mouth. The food is carried to certain organs where it undergoes a chemical change. Afterwards, it is taken up by the bloodstream and utilized by the red corpuscles for building purposes.

In the termitary, food is taken through several foramina and roughly chewed. It is then carried to different centres. A certain kind of termite then transforms it chemically. Next, it enters the living stream and is used as food for the different members of the community and for building purposes. With a magnifying glass, you can observe how each termite uses a drop of fluid from its own body to cover each minute grain which is used for building. This fluid holds the structure together. Most of the water used is carried up the vertical shaft leading from subterranean sources of moisture.

At this point, it is necessary to discuss normal and abnormal growth from another angle.

Physical growth is the most perfect example in nature of the psyche of inherited memory. It always appears very wonderful and inexplicable. Humans use their own consciousness as a criterion for classification. Eventually, we discover that this consciousness can never be a criterion for psychological processes different from our own. We are inclined, for instance, to be amazed at the abnormal functioning of the subconscious mind. The subconscious mind is no more than the rudimentary animal psyche still present in humans. In the same way, we are amazed at our own physical growth. However, our criteria are proven to be false once we study similar phenomena in nature and begin to classify our knowledge.

We tend to believe that the psyche, which directs human growth, is something far beyond our own comprehension. It would appear capable of performing miracles and to have some purpose far beyond our own understanding. Strangely enough, the psyche which directs physical growth is, in some respects, more ignorant than the psyche of a child. Even the 'roadmaker' ant which was recently discussed would take years to learn that twice two always makes four, and is a genius compared to this psyche. The psyche of physical growth comes lowest in the scale when 'learn by experience' is our rule of measure. If you take *reasoning* powers as your measure, this psyche comes even lower.

When you realize that the same psyche which will, from its own experience, never learn that two and two make four, can, beginning with a single cell, build up an elephant or a person, or an oak tree, cell by cell, then the process may become confusing. That is because you use different measures.

One measure alone cannot be used for classification. Hence, abnormal growth is often perpetuated, in spite of constant destruction through the underlying weakness of structure – just as we saw in the termites with their tower. This would be the case too, if for example, it was discovered that in every elephant, every human, every oak tree, there were parts which were built 'wrongly' – for instance, if you were to find elephants with five legs, with deformed jaws, with regular but abnormal cell structures which form a danger to the whole body.

The realization that one system of classification does not apply across the board leads to another important conclusion. Every psychologist who studies the group soul in nature seeks an answer to the question: *is there some powerful group soul above and beyond nature which dominates all natural phenomena and directs them to some goal?*

Searching for an answer in nature seems impossible. If a naturalist is truthful, and not unduly influenced by a desired outcome, then the ability to give a final answer will always be in question. It is possible that we see only a small arc of a gigantic circle. A true understanding of the universal soul lies far beyond our human abilities.

It may be stated that the purpose of life is natural development. It may be assumed that evolution leads to a state of absolute perfection, not relative perfection. All that development does, however, is to equip the organism to withstand the enemies that assail it in a specific environment.

For every new 'weapon' it receives, it must lay down an old one. In other words, as one skill is developed, another becomes less refined. Humans are the most developed psychologically, yet a high price has been paid for the psyche of individual causal memory. We have seen that the psyche, which directs growth, possesses traces of the powers of learning by experience, of reasoning or of intelligence. In all circumstances, nature is harsh. The environment does not take into account the vast range of human emotions. It doesn't allow for any protection of the weak or vulnerable.

The psyche attains its highest pinnacle in the higher mammals – that is, humanity. This would indicate that there is some purpose in nature, whose guiding principle is a psyche similar, but infinitely more developed, than the soul of the primate. If this is the case, it is virtually impossible to find evidence in our natural surroundings. Consequently, we are as equally unable to understand such an exalted psyche as the termite has a chance of comprehending humanity.

*

If nature possesses a universal psyche, it is one far above the common and strongest feelings of the human psyche. Nature is inescapably harsh, relentless and ruthless. She has certainly never wept in sympathy, nor stretched a hand protectively over even the most beautiful or innocent of her creatures.

8

The Development of the Composite Animal

IT HAS NOW BEEN CLEARLY ESTABLISHED that the termitary is a separate and composite animal in exactly the same way that a person is a separate and composite animal. The primary difference is the power of movement. However, there are also other animals which do have not the power of movement. It is necessary to grasp these biological phenomena in order to understand the life history of the termite.

All this may remind you of the mountain in labour, which eventually produced a very small mouse. The facts I have given, however, are as strictly true as any other established biological phenomenon, and it is necessary to accept them if you wish to understand the life history of the termite.

If you make a small, round vertical hole with a stick, for instance in the round termitary made by *Eutermes* (later called *Trinervitertnes*) – and then isolate the wound with a sharp circular cut through the skin, the termites begin to repair the wound. What you have done causes in many cases a curious reflex. The termites begin abnormal building. Instead of repairing the cells and passages and growing a new skin over the wound, they build a tower.

The stimulus is believed to be the entry of sunlight. If the base is too small, the tower topples over, again and again, as soon as it reaches a certain height, and just as often, the termites reconstruct it. The tower is not only unnecessary to the termitary, but actually a distinct disadvantage.

It is a disturbing influence which throws the normal course of life of the organism into disorder. It is similar to the growth of a cancer.

As an example, catch a pair of our common house lizards and tame them. With a blade, make two or three longitudinal cuts in the tail. In some cases, you will cause a curious reflex and an abnormal growth will begin. Instead of merely repairing the wound, a new tail is grown. If you amputate the new tail, you may find a double tail sprouting. In this way, you can – if all goes well – manufacture a lizard with seven tails. In the same way, we can manufacture a termitary with seven towers, to the great disadvantage of the whole community. We cannot make a lizard's tail; nor can we make a tower with the same materials and in the same way as the termite.

*

If this theory is borne in mind, ample proof will be evident when the termite is studied. The insects themselves should always be thought of as the bloodstream and organs of a single animal.

If the highly developed, highly specialized animals originally developed from communities such as the termite, one should be able to find instances of such symbiosis – which is more than mere partnership – low down in the scale of organic life.

There are many such instances which justify the belief that organisms of several kinds can result from a successful amalgamation. An example of this is the union between fungus and algae to form a lichen, which differs enormously from both original entities.

The results of the process are far more clearly seen, however, higher in the animal kingdom. In the sea around the African coast, there can be found a hundred kinds of a certain species of marine creature. Its scientific name is *Hydromedusa*, and there is a related species known as *Siphonophora*.

In the instance of the *Siphonophora*, there is no other animal of its size in the ocean which can boast such an extensive bibliography. Ernst Hackel and other famous naturalists spent years studying, describing and classifying them. The great peculiarity of these creatures is that every full-grown specimen is a composite animal composed of hundreds of individuals.

These individuals are born by a budding process from the generative group of the composite animal. These newly born individuals swim round freely and are able to continue life singly and reproduce themselves. Each is a perfect marine creature with mouth, stomach, swimming apparatus and sexual organs.

If by chance a group of *Siphonophora* happens to meet, they cling to each other. In some species, an organic union immediately takes place, while in others it is something less than this. Apart from this small difference, the final result is the same. Immediately after the union, the single individuals undergo an interesting change.

One group forms a complicated swimming apparatus; another group becomes the stomach and digestive system; and yet another group develops into the sexual organs of the composite animal. One group even takes on hepatic functions, and becomes the liver. Each individual of such a group loses all its separate organic functions. Those of the stomach group, for instance, forget they ever sought food or had a sexual life of their own. The new organism is a perfect whole animal. If it was viewed in its perfect stage, you would not believe that it had been formed in this way from separate individuals.

Yet one can break it up again! One can tear apart the composite animal until it becomes completely disorganized. You might expect that death would be the result, but this is not the case. Each individual organism begins to stir in the water. Slowly, it repairs its lost organs and functions, until at last, it is once again a perfect individual. It is now as different from the composite *Siphonophora* as the camel is from a whale. One can repeat this process innumerable times, without apparently injuring either the individual or the composite creature.

In such a way, our termitary has been formed; in the same way the individuals have undergone wonderful changes in order to form group organs. In every termitary, there is a brain, a stomach, a liver and sexual organs which ensure the propagation of the race. They have legs and arms for gathering food; they have a mouth. If natural selection continues to operate, the final result could be a termitary which moves slowly over the *veld*!

There are hundreds of facts, biological and psychological, in nature which suggest that all highly developed animals have been formed from separate organisms. I once collected many such facts and classified them, hoping to startle the scientific world. Unfortunately, my 'tower' collapsed, not because it was wrongly built, but because other naturalists had already become aware of all this. Claude Bernard, in his opening address to the French Academy (1869) and Dr Durand Gos, in his *Electrodynamique Vitale* (1855) and *Variétés Philosophiques* (1857), tried to show that the vital organs of people were separate animals.

At the time of my own research, Jean Finot, in his optimistic demonstration on life and death, wrote:

> "The teaching that the human organism is composed of separate animals, each with a separate system, will, we hope, find more and more proof in the scientific investigation of our time."

Another fact one should constantly remember is that if there is any truth in this theory of development, then just as certainly, the termite was originally a perfect flying individual insect, of which the queen and king are the prototypes. The union of these individuals and the wonderful changes which resulted from it is a late development in the history of the species. If the blind, wingless, sexless soldiers and workers are not a degeneration of the perfect king and queen type, then, the opposite conclusion will have to be accepted: the perfect king and queen must be a development from one or other of the sexless types, and yet that cannot be the case. There are other biological facts which indicate that the imperfect types are the result of degenerative change of the perfect insect. The rudiments of wing buds and of sexual organs in the sexless types show clearly the direction in which development, or rather degeneration, has gone.

This mound is home to a colony of grass eating termites, Nasutitermes triodiae. It is about 15 feet high and could be over 50 years old.

9

The Birth of the Termite Community

U NTIL THIS POINT, the termites and the termitary have been observed from without. The termitary and the growth and life history of the termites will now be studied from within the nest. Every step will prove to be a surprise; as many things will be revealed that seem incredible. The termite differs in every respect from all other insects.

Morphologically, there is little in nature which reminds us of the termite; that is, their form and structure, independent from their function. Their ontological development is also a constant surprise. In terms of its phylogenetic development – its race history – it is necessary to look to the ocean for a corresponding pattern of development. The entomologist who studied the termite for the first time would be justified in viewing it as an immigrant from a different planet.

The wings of the termite alone are worthy of mention. Where can one find in nature an organism which, during its own lifetime, will yield up the mightiest of all weapons in the struggle for life – its wings? This abandonment of wings is an example of the surprises with which the termite constantly confronts us.

In recalling the different inmates of a Transvaal termitary, it is hard to believe that they are the children of one father and one mother. We have seen how the kings and queens leave the nest in swarms; how they *must* fly to unlock their sexual life; how the queen sends a signal; how both sexes discard their wings as soon as they reach the ground after their one and only flight.

The development of the wings is very interesting. In the sexual type, one can see the wing buds quite early in life. When the insect has shed its skin for the last time and is fully grown, the wings begin to grow from these buds with a kind of hinge which allows for the greatest possible range of movements. It is from this hinge that the insect breaks its wings with a lightning-like movement after its flight. It takes hold of the wing buds with the nearest pair of legs, which appear to be specially adapted for this purpose, shifts them along the bud until they reach the hinge, and detaches the wings.

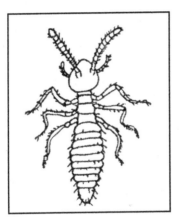

Trinervitermes. Etiolated, newly hatched termite.
Colour: White. All classes and both sexes are found. Sex organs are rudimentary, disappearing as development proceeds. Entirely blind. In some individuals, rudimentary pigmented spots are found in place of eyes. These, too, disappear. In others, rudimentary wing-buds appear, which never develop.

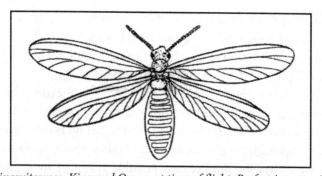

Trinervitermes. King and Queen at time of flight. Perfect insects with fully developed eyes, wings and sex organs. Colour: Dark brown, with red markings. Highly pigmented. Functions: 1. Reproduction. 2. Analogous to motor and sensory centres of brain in higher animals.

When they have been shed, one can find no wound to indicate the spot of attachment, as might be expected. There must be some organic union, there must be some attachment to the central system which enables the wings to be set into motion. However, there is no sign of this immediately after the wings are detached. It is a mystery how such a complicated organ, which is so powerful and which is under the complete control of the insect, can give such little evidence of organic union with the body. One moment, the insect is flying, a moment later the wings are detached, yet one finds no evidence of a lesion.

Another interesting point is that the insect appears to be able to discard the wings by a voluntary movement of the wing itself. Before flight has taken place, she will struggle to free herself, if she is held by the wings, without the wings becoming detached. If, however, she has experienced the sensation of flight – and even *one* movement of the wings appears to be sufficient to satisfy the instinct – then she will discard the wings in someone's hand.

The observer must understand that it is *absolutely* necessary for her future life that she shall at least experience the impression of flight. If she has not, she simply dies. Then

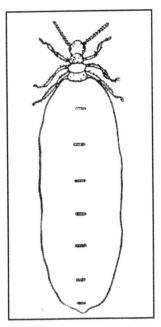

Bellicosus. Queen. Beginning of second stage of development.
Functions: Female element in reproduction. Sensory and motor
aspects of the 'brain'. As in the higher animals, the female element
of the termitary undergoes periodical metamorphosis and has a far
greater ontogenetic development than the male.

she will never become a queen and her sexual life is ended. Sometimes even the struggle for freedom as her wings are held is sufficient to satisfy the instinct. Rapid and continuous movement of the wings, while the insect remains stationary on a twig without actual flight through the air, also appears to satisfy it occasionally. These occurrences are more an exception, rather than a rule. As a rule, there is complete frustration sexually if the insect has not flown and discarded her wings.

The king and queen look exactly alike and cannot be distinguished with the naked eye. They are the only perfectly formed insects in the termitary. They have fully developed eyes, and although they were born and reared in darkness,

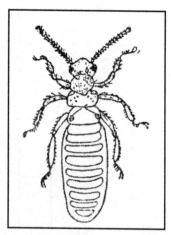

Bellicosus. Queen substitute. Similar to Queen or King type, except that the wings do not develop. Function: Sometimes used temporarily as a substitute for the king or queen. Both sexes found.

they are highly pigmented. Black, brown and red colourings are evident which never appear in their children, except of course the future kings and queens.

The sexual organs are fully developed. Any natural means of defence is surprisingly lacking. There is probably no insect in South Africa which has so many natural enemies. It is possible to find the true ant, not the termite, walking round boldly in the daylight, for only reptiles – such as frogs and lizards – which have no sense of taste try to eat them. Their defence consists of an acid which is secreted for the purpose, and also an indigestible outer covering. So effective apparently are these methods of defence that we find certain beetles taking on the form of large ants so successfully that most animals are deceived by them.

The unfortunate termite, on the other hand, is greedily eaten by many other animals. It is a remarkable experience to watch the flight of the termites in uninhabited parts of Central Africa. Within a few minutes, the surface of the earth is seething with living creatures coming to the feast. Out of the earth crawl frogs, toads, snakes, lizards and other reptiles. It is not possible to tell how they are aware that a feast of termites is available. Even the tortoise appears. Other insects, crickets, beetles, centipedes, spiders and scorpions all swarm in the grass. In the water, just below the surface, you can see hundreds of fish and turtles. Out of the bushes, jackals, cats, meercats, apes and monkeys appear. There is a temporary truce, except in the case of the unfortunate flying termites. They appear to be going to fly merely to die.

This provides an understanding of why nature produces them in such millions, notwithstanding the fact that each pair may be the origin of millions more. Every pair is necessary, because the slaughter is immense. It is now clear why the royal pair are in such a tremendous hurry after they have flown and discarded their wings. The only method of defence the flying termites make use of is flight after dusk. In this way, they escape at least the birds which fly by day. Even this may not always happen. Sometimes, the flight begins too early and in the twilight, hundreds of hawks gather. The nighthawks, owls and other night birds continue the feast into the darkest hours of the night.

In this case, there has been a displacement of the natural means of defence. What the individual king and queen have lost as regards their natural means of defence is compensated for by the defences of the composite animal, the termitary. As soon as the community is formed, the termites never again appear in the daylight. The only exception is when injury necessitates this, and even then, it is not in great numbers. However far they may have to go in search of food, and sometimes it may be hundreds of yards, they make underground passages in all directions. The food itself is temporarily covered with cells and earthwork, making it unnecessary for any individual to appear in the open.

The same thing occurs with all other psychological characteristics and urges – they are shifted from the individual to the community. The individual termite is without feeling. For the termite, there is no more pain. The injury of a group of termites, however, is felt as pain by the entire community. The same thing occurs in the human body. The liver is incapable of feeling an injury. It is the human being, the composite animal, which becomes aware of the injury to the liver as pain.

Neither does the individual termite feel hunger or thirst. If there is a famine, or if water begins getting scarce, the suffering, as such, is felt only in the queen's chamber.

The mightiest urge of all, the sexual urge, does not exist in the individual. It has been set free from this demand. The only element of autonomy which appears to exist amongst the termites are the food, damage, and danger signals which are sent out by the soldiers and answered by the workers. Nevertheless, this is still not proof that the individual termite possesses a separate psyche. Apart from the power of movement, there is no trace of such a psyche; all motivations are directed by signals from the queen's chamber.

These signals immediately cease if the queen is destroyed. All directed activity ceases, even in the outlying sections of the termitary. This includes those sections that have been completely isolated over a long period by a metal plate. This seems to provide proof that the group movements also are directed by the queen, the brain of the termitary.

The king and queen, deep in the absolute darkness of their chamber, bear in their persons two widely diverse functions; the mental and the sexual. The palace chamber is analogous to the skull in higher animals. Even the substance of the queen's body is reminiscent of the brain of mammals. All that is entirely lacking are the nerves, which play such an important role in the physical economy of the more highly developed animals.

The conclusion has now been established that the termitary is a composite animal. As such, it may also be assumed that it would be possible to find some trace at least of nerve structures.

Further consideration shows that none of the kind is actually found. The most important function in the human species of the nerves is that of initiating and controlling movement, and to carry impressions from the sense organs to the brain.

On the other hand, there are innumerable movements and functions in the human body which are directed and influenced by the brain without being connected to the nervous system. This 'influence at a distance' is found all over the body. The work and movements of the blood corpuscles, for instance, are activated by an influence which is not material. This is similar to the special functions of the vital organs. The influence which streams from the queen is something intangible and similar to the 'influence at a distance' which directs so many functions in highly developed animals.

This mysterious influence has the power of penetrating all ordinary materials. For instance, it penetrates quite easily the thickest obtainable galvanized iron plates. Distance, however, lessens the power of the queen's influence. One can imagine nature addressing the queen after her short flight:

> "Beloved, you are going to suffer a great loss. Instead of living in this glowing sunlight, you are going to spend your days in absolute darkness. Instead of the citizenship of the wide *veld*, instead of the freedom of the air, of mountains, trees and plains, you are going to spend your days as a prisoner in a narrow vault, in whose confines you will be unable to make the least movement. The annual return of the love season, the search for your beloved and the happy finding of your home and all the happiness bound up in this periodical stirring of the soul, of all this you are to be deprived.
>
> But in place of all this, you yourself will become a far more important and wonderful being. Although you will apparently be an immobile shapeless mass buried in a living grave, you

> will actually be a sensitive mainspring. You will
> become the feeling, the thinking, the seeing, of a
> life a thousand times greater and more important
> than yours could ever have become.
>
> Above all, I will give you protection. The million
> dangers, the million enemies which threatened
> your life on every hand, will in your new life fling
> themselves in vain against your armour."

It was this need for protection which caused the development of the termitary. As individuals, the queen and her subjects are the most threatened of all insects. As individuals, in an unprotected environment, the species would never have survived. But as a composite animal, the termitary is very nearly perfectly protected. External wounds and destructive attacks, which destroy the whole visible form of the termitary, do not touch its real life. This goes on as usual, as though nothing unusual has happened. The wounds are merely repaired. The queen herself, as the brain of the organism, is as well protected as the human brain in its skull. There are very few enemies which ever prove a real danger to the queen. One of the largest is the ant-eater; while some of the most insidious are groups of beetles, which at times completely devastate a weakened termitary. This example is comparable in every respect to the attack on the human body by pathological organisms. The termitary becomes diseased and dies.

Has the queen paid too dearly for protection? Nature answers this question in a different way from that in which we, or the queen, would.

> "What matters it to me how much or how little
> is paid for the privilege of my protection? How
> much happiness is lost and how much misery the
> new life entails is of no importance. What do I
> care for the individual? The race is safe, rejoicing,
> inexterminable. The individual must always pay,
> and no price is too high."

It is clear why development has taken this strange course, and why at all costs the queen must remain immobile, why she has been imprisoned in a cell, and has lost all power of movement. If she is the brain of the organism, that makes it all the more necessary for her to remain stationary in one place.

The duplicate mental and sexual functions of the queen make things even more complicated. Movement appears to be an integral part of all sexual functions in nature. There seems to be a definite conflict here, but the development of the termitary has solved the problem.

A further explanation of this duplication of function in the termites is evident in an examination of the same, less developed complex in the bee queen. In the case of the bee, the sexual functions are the most important, and the result is that the danger of the queen on her wedding flight becomes a danger to the whole hive. The termite queen is never again exposed to such danger, once the community is formed and she has been rendered immobile.

The human observer who watched the flight of the queen, who saw the glad meeting of the two sexes, who perhaps even lent a little human aid, gives a sigh of relief when eventually the threatened pair find shelter in the protective lap of Mother Earth. Now at last they must be safe. Alas! Not yet.

There is another great danger which threatens the birth of the new community. In South Africa, it is an ongoing enemy – drought. The termites must have water, more water, and still more water. As ninety per cent of their bodies consists of water, the greatest part of their labour is concerned with the finding and carrying of water. The termitary is just as dependent as the warm-blooded animals are on water for survival. The king and queen must find water immediately. They obtain this from damp earth. That is why the flight occurs only after heavy rains – this at least they expect from the environment to ensure their survival. Sometimes, however, they make a mistake.

The first duty of the royal pair is to manufacture an organ

for hatching and feeding the first workers and soldiers. For this purpose, a plentiful supply of water is necessary. If the water supply fails during this initial period, all is finished; it means death to them and to the composite animal. Both king and queen work incessantly, making passages in the direction of moist earth. These generally descend perpendicularly and are the beginnings of the vertical aqueduct – at least in dry districts. It is here they make their first termite gardens when at intervals in these first passages they make, or perhaps find, hollows in the earth. Observers of the real ant have called them 'gardens', so it is appropriate to continue using the term. They are similar to the agricultural practices of our own society.

First, the ground is carefully prepared. The fertilizer consists of finely chewed, partially digested vegetable material, mostly dry wood and grass stalks. Then it is irrigated with a huge amount of water, until the ground is saturated. Both the king and queen labour incessantly; they do not rest for a second, nor do they sleep, day or night. It is the last time, however, that they will ever be expected to work. The functions which they will fulfil in the future can hardly be called 'work', compared to that of the worker and soldier termites.

At last, the first garden is ready, deep in a hollow of one of the passages. It is essential that no rays of light must ever fall upon it or penetrate it. Everything is done in complete darkness.

This first garden consists of a pat of cell structure and earthwork. When it is well saturated, the two termites proceed to plant the seeds of a strange fungus. This will play an enormous role in the future life of the termitary, and therefore requires careful attention. While it has been said that the termites plant the seed, this cannot be proven. It is however, what appears to take place. They walk about on the damp garden and in the shortest possible time necessary for germination and development, the fungus springs up, in the form of a white mould. The hyphae and spores of the fungus have actually

A fungus garden

been found on the jaws and legs of flying termites immediately after they have left the termitary. It appears as though they purposely carry the seed to plant in the new nest. It is also possible to find spores on termites which have nothing to do with the gardens. In the neighbourhood of large termitaries, spores may be found in great numbers in the underground hollows and passages. They are spread by water, by wind, by worms and by insects. It is possible, therefore, that the spores might establish themselves on the specially prepared ground, without the assistance of the termite. The termites, however, do far more incredible things than the planting of these spores would be. It is thus reasonable to assume that they do carry the spores, and that the planting of the gardens is intentional.

Whether they do actually plant seed or not, there is certainly no question about the fertilization and irrigation of the gardens. The passage which leads to the water is constantly being deepened. While the damp earth is being excavated, the moisture is stored in the bodies of the two insects. The garden is irrigated with drops of a clear shining liquid. This liquid is the same in all respects as that which is used for many other purposes later on by all the groups.

In this early garden, the queen lays her first eggs. At this stage, she is still able to run about quickly and work actively. Meanwhile, amazing things are happening to the fungus garden. The two insects do something to the mycelium of the plant. This retards growth and development, and at the same time, the temperature of the garden begins to rise astoundingly.

At first, the origin of this rise in temperature seems inexplicable. It cannot come from the termites, for their bodies are always at the same temperature as that of their environment. It in fact comes from the garden, which functions as an incubator. It is responsible for later maintaining the heat of the composite animal. The normal temperature of the termitary, taken in the queen's cell, is from four to six degrees Fahrenheit higher than the normal temperature of a human being. There

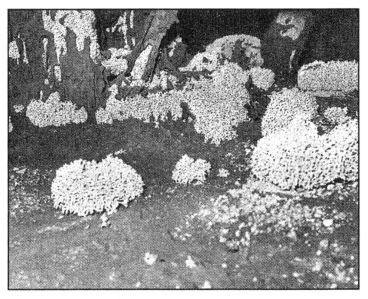

A termitary split open to reveal the fungus gardens

Termite damage in structural timber

is little doubt that most of this heat is generated by the fungus-beds. It is well known that in all fungi a rise in temperature takes place when the spores ripen. In the gardens of the termitary, the temperature is kept raised to a certain degree by something the termite does to the plant. This function retards growth and development at the very stage when the fungi generate most heat. The garden, therefore, acts as more than an incubator and nursery. The production of heat is certainly a very important function, but in addition to this, the garden also becomes the stomach and liver of the composite animal.

By constant and rapid metabolism, not only nutriment but also digestive juices are assembled in the fungus. Under the microscope, and chemically, you can find oil, protoplasm, glycogen, carbohydrates, proteid crystals, gum, alkaloids, and different enzymes. These are similar to those in the human body which break up complicated sugars into dextrose and levulose. These in turn reduce ordinary sugar to alcohol and carbon. The only substance of which there is no trace is starch.

The circle of digestion takes place in the following way: the workers, and the king and queen in their first stages, are the only termites in the nest which can chew wood, grass-stalks and other coarse vegetable matter, and partially digest it. No other group in the termitary is able to absorb or digest anything but fluid. When the king and queen in their first stage, or the workers, have partially digested the food, it goes to the stomach and liver – the so-called gardens. Here it is further digested and changed by the fungi and the digestive juices. It happens in just the same way as in the human body. When the stomach and liver have prepared the food, it is taken up by the workers and soldiers in liquid form, and becomes part of the whole circulation.

More than half of this predigested food is used for building purposes. If you touch a newly built tower, your fingers become sticky. With a magnifying glass, you can see how each worker rolls a tiny grain of soil in its jaws, coating it with sticky fluid before placing it in position. This is the fluid which is obtained from the gardens. The water necessary for the production of this fluid is being constantly supplied to the gardens by a stream of workers. Their sole function appears to be this supply of water and the sowing of seed. If a vertical aqueduct is present, you can find a hollow every two or three feet, in which a small garden is cultivated. During severe droughts, water is constantly carried to the deepest gardens, and the fungi there are kept alive. The great advantage of having little fungus beds so near to the water spares the termites considerable labour. From these gardens, the seed is carried to new ones, or to replant those which were killed by drought. These smaller gardens are never used for any other purpose. That is, you will never find them used as nurseries, as is the case with the large gardens.

Another function of the fungus gardens appears to be the isolation of colour. A dark-red colouring material can be obtained from them. It appears, therefore, that the termites find the red colouring matter of their bodies prepared for them by the gardens. The babies are entirely colourless, as one would expect from insects born in utter darkness. One would expect that they would never become coloured in the absence of light, and as they continue living in darkness, it is difficult to explain the presence of all the brilliant tints. These, however, appear to come from the gardens. The babies are as white as milk, until they are fed on the fungus fluid. It is only then that we find their bodies assuming the blood-red colour of the adults.

10
Pain and Travail in Nature

IT IS NOW IMPORTANT to observe the conjugal behaviour of the king and queen in more detail. There are three exceptional phenomena. The word 'wonderful' does not fit into science, for from one point of view, every natural occurrence is as wonderful as another. In this case, though, we are justified in using the term when we meet a phenomenon which is such an exception to the ordinary rules of nature that it appears to be a miracle.

The early behaviour of the king and queen is a phenomenon of this kind. There is a hidden meaning that has escaped even the most experienced of observers. The naturalist Grassi studied these phenomenon in very favourable circumstances, but he was not able to ascertain their meaning.

Scientific study depends to a large extent on the particular aspect that the observer is interested in. If behaviour is the focus, and you possess some knowledge of it, you will focus on many aspects that the entomologist will overlook. In this instance, the powers of observation are trained to notice form; naming and classifying are the objective; so that to an entomologist, the dead insect is often of more worth than the living one. This does not mean that this work is of less importance. It may even be of greater value than pure psychological investigation. If, however, these things escape the experienced entomologist, it is even more necessary to be aware of these elements.

Up to the moment when the first garden has been made and planted and the first eggs laid, the two insects, the king and queen, ordinary four-winged neuropterous insects, have been busy building their home. They have been laying eggs, just like thousands of other insects around them. While they have laid aside their wings, they still continue to behave like normal insects.

Then, however, strange things begin happening. These events are so extraordinary that it is hard to believe they actually occur.

While the queen is laying her eggs, the searchlight we use for our studies disturbs her less than at any other time. It seems that her important work occupies her attention so deeply that even a momentous event such as the sudden flashing of a torch does not frighten her.

Her preparations are both fascinating and perplexing. For a long while before she begins laying, she stands on the place where the eggs are to be deposited. Her body is in constant movement. Her antennae sweep in circles and her jaws move ceaselessly. Occasionally, she lifts the hind part of her body in just the same way as she did when she was sending her first signal to her mate. Two or three times before the eggs are actually laid, she turns round and looks at the ground as if she expects to find something there.

With the actual laying of the eggs, the bodily contractions increase significantly. When the first batch is laid, she turns round once more, and examines them long and carefully. She touches them gently with her jaws and front legs, and then she lies motionless beside them for a time. What does it all mean?

We are here observing one of those 'wonders' which is found in no other winged insect, nor in any other insect of similar development. Unless you have witnessed a similar occurrence in an animal a little higher in the scale of life, it is not possible to realize the significance of this behaviour. We have in fact, witnessed the first appearance of a complex which plays a mighty role in the decadent and unnatural condition of the human race today. This is the first evidence in nature of birth pangs. It is certainly hard to grasp that this may be the case in a winged insect. Surely, it must be impossible. How can one tell that the queen's behaviour is due to pain?

What usually happens in insects is this: the female builds a home, fills it with food, lays her eggs as easily as if she were eating, drinking or cleaning her antennae. The male never appears on the scene. After the honeymoon, his part of the work is done. The female's work also ends with the building of the house and the laying of the eggs. She never sees her babies. She would not recognize them if she did, for how could she, a beautiful, flying creature, have given birth to these odd little grubs, or wriggling worms?

In actual fact, a 'real' insect baby has never been seen. You would expect it to be a caterpillar, then a cocoon, from which eventually comes the *imago*, the perfect insect, which does not differ from the parent. But a little white insect baby is found in the termite world which does not undergo any further metamorphosis. It is born weak and helpless, and slowly grows stronger, just like a human baby. It is doubtful whether there is a similar occurrence anywhere else in the insect world?

There are instances of this, but never in an insect at the same stage of development as the termite queen. The South African scorpion is zoologically classified among the insects, but psychologically should be in the mammal class.

Among my tame scorpions, there was a gigantic female which gained a good deal of fame. She was five and a half inches long. The following is a case study.

> She first introduced herself to Mr Charlie Pienaar by killing a fully grown chicken in his presence. She tackled the chicken's leg, clung on, and gave one sting of her deadly lance, just above the joint. Within a few seconds, the chicken was paralysed and was dead in ten minutes.

Later on, she became so tame and knew me so well, that I could suddenly push a finger before her, and allow her to grip me with her claws. She would bring her sting into contact with my skin, before recognizing me. Immediately, she would relax and withdraw her dangerous weapon. I could handle her freely. She liked being gently scratched.

Shortly after she came into my possession, I noticed that an interesting event was shortly to take place. I watched her continually and gave her every care, for I wished to observe every stage of the process. I must admit that in those days I knew so little zoology that I expected to see her lay eggs. I was astounded therefore to see her give birth to sixteen living babies. Fully harnessed and spurred they made their entry by pairs, small white helpless babies – but perfect little scorpions. There was no doubt at all that the delivery caused the mother much pain. I remember a woman asking me anxiously whether the young ones were born with pincers and stings, and then giving a prayer of thanks that human babies at least do not possess those.

What seemed very strange, too, was that the scorpion mother loved her strange little youngsters. Very carefully she helped them on to her back, where they remained sitting in two rows with their heads and pincers directed outwards and their tails interlaced behind them. I knew her well enough to tell by her behaviour that she would not allow any handling of her babies, so I did not risk doing this until they were fully grown. The mother would tear their food into small pieces and feed them carefully, while above them she waved her sting defensively. A more loving mother you will find nowhere else in nature.

As a result of this study, it immediately seemed that this was yet another instance of examining one of nature's deepest mysteries. This example also highlighted that there are still many boundaries to explore in terms of assessing the validity of existing theories. In relation to the appearance of pain in nature, no satisfactory explanation has yet been given. Many theories have been formulated, some of them probably bordering on the truth, but in my experience, I don't know any naturalist who has given a well-grounded, true analysis of the subject. Those who have, by original research, even approached the secret of birth pain can be counted on the fingers of one hand.

It is apparent that birth pain is a great mystery. One knows that pain in general is a warning signal to living creatures. If pain were to disappear from this earth, life would soon cease. Without pain, organic matter cannot exist. Everywhere in nature, pain acts as a defence – except in the case of birth. Why then do we find this agony of suffering at the birth of highly developed animals? It plays such an important part, and is so common, that it must have some equally important purpose. What purpose has natural selection played in allowing this amazing exception to the general rule? Birth pain is clearly not protective; indeed, it is the very opposite.

It is often possible to most effectively learn the meaning of normal phenomena by observing what happens in unnatural and abnormal manifestations of the same thing. One knows that in apes, in tame animals and in humans, the mechanism which causes birth pains may be a danger to the lives of both mother and child. Yet birth is the great end of the struggle for existence – the event which nature, as it were, considers the first and most important, and which it would protect with all her powers, and make safe for both mother and child.

Why should it be coupled with violent and non-protective suffering, which increases as you mount the scale of life? What does this mean?

With an ordinary immersion lens dipped in a drop of stagnant water from a cattle *kraal*, it is possible to observe life with an immersion lens, without stain or oil. I watched the movements of *Volvox* and *Amoeba* for hours on end. It was interesting to note that many unnatural conditions in their environment may be created. For instance, a red-hot needle pressed against the glass will cause a sudden rise in the temperature of the water film. This is enough to cause the death of a unicellular organism. It is also possible to introduce strychnine, carbolic acid, or arsenic over the outer edge of the film. A strong ray of red light, sharper than a needle point, played over the film will also kill the organisms. From these experiments, certain insights may be gained. You can see the unicellular animals start to retract from the dangers you have caused. If you study similar instances in higher animals, you find that nature guards the way to death with pain.

On the unaffected side of your film, you can see the cells budding, dividing and multiplying.

It was once stated that all behaviourism in nature could be linked to hunger. While this claim has been repeated thousands of times, it is actually false. Hunger itself is pain – the most severe pain, in its later stages, that the body knows, except for thirst, which is even worse. The emotion of love may be regarded as a hunger, but it is not pain.

What protects animals, what enables them to continue living, what assures the propagation of the species? It is a certain attribute of organic matter, for as soon as life is identified, this attribute is evident. It is inherent in life; and like most natural phenomena, it is polarized; that is, there is a negative and a positive pole. The negative pole is pain; the positive pole is sex. This attribute may be called the saving attribute of life. This is the closest to what appears to be a common purpose in nature.

All animals, large and small, possess some mechanism

for feeling pain. This pain always acts as a safeguard against death. An animal struggles to get out of the water, not because it is afraid of death – of which it knows nothing – but because the first stages of drowning are painful and distressing. Close to the pole of pain, we find fear as another urge that leads to certain behaviour. The other pole, sex, is more complicated – the final result of it is mother love.

In the apes – in a lesser degree – and in humans – in the highest degree – there has been a great degeneration of both poles. In humans, there no longer exists any selective power against the attack of pathological organisms and thousands of organic diseases. The result is that the mechanism of pain, which developed only as a defence in nature, is ineffectually brought into action. It is a result of the ills that are inherent to humanity, and from which animals in natural environments are free.

Sex has become degenerate in people to the same degree. In nature, the sexual urge, like other race memories, needs an external stimulus before it is roused. As we have seen, this is scent alone in most mammals. Sometimes scent and colour are paired. In such cases, we find brilliant colourings in the female as well as scent. In such animals, destruction of the olfactory sense in the male means the end of sex.

In the ape and humanity, we find the first animals, excluding tame animals, in which sex can be roused without an external stimulus. The reason for this is one that has been previously discussed. In humans and apes, all perceptions and all experiences are registered as individual causal memories. The cortex of the brain is the organ of this function. The first awareness of sex must be transmitted through the cortex, as an ordinary causal environmental memory. It is then immediately absorbed as a separate memory. The ape, and humans, remember this as a pleasurable experience to which they can react at will. The result is that the greatest of all natural laws, periodicity, is lost in the human race. The periodic organic condition, which should rouse the sexual sense, has become a redundant, degenerate, pathological manifestation. The ultimate result, birth, which in all other animals is assured, has become in the human a major surgical operation, where the lives of both mother and child may be endangered.

As a German obstetrician stated:

> " Without skilled help in labour, the civilized races would vanish from the earth in three generations. Two-thirds of all the organic and mental disease of humanity may be ascribed to the degeneracy of the sexual sense."

A little way behind humans, we find apes, with similar degeneracy and similar results, only to a lesser extent.

We have taken a brief and general glance at the two poles, pain and sex. There still remains the mysterious exception – that is, birth pain. It is however, clear that this has no connection with protective pain. It does not provide any protection leading to death; as no animal can escape from it.

We have learnt the general rule that every instinctive action is unlocked by one, and only one, key. We have seen how in the termite the stimulus or key to sex is flight, and in the kudu, scent; and how the entire aquatic life of the otter is initiated by the sight and touch of water. In exactly the same way, we find that birth pain is the key which unlocks the door to mother love, in all animals from the termite queen to the whale. Where pain is negligible, mother love and care are feeble. Where pain is absent, there is absolutely no mother love.

During ten years of observation, I did not find a single exception to this rule. A naturalist once suggested that the function of birth pain was to draw the attention of the mother to the child in her care. This is not so. There is no such thing as 'drawing attention' in the instinctive soul. The unlocking of the mother love complex through pain is beyond consciousness. It is beyond the knowledge of the mother, and has nothing to do with drawing her attention to her offspring. However, it was not sufficient to show the connection between birth pain and mother love, in order to prove that one was the result of the other. A large number of experiments dispelled all doubt. The following notes will explain the general principle.

For the experiment, I used a herd of 60 half-wild buck, known in South Africa as Kaffir Buck. I have proof that, during the previous fifteen years, there had been no single instance of a mother refusing her young in normal circumstances.

1) Six cases of birth during full anaesthesia of the mother induced by chloroform and ether; unconsciousness in no case lasted for more than 25 minutes after delivery. In all six cases, the mother refused to accept the lamb of her own will.

2) Four cases of birth during paralysis – consciousness and feeling were partly paralysed, but not destroyed, by the American arrow poison curare. In all four cases, the mother appeared for over an hour to be in great doubt as to the acceptance of her lamb. After this period, three mothers accepted their lambs while one refused it.

To prove that refusal on the part of these mothers was not to the general disturbance caused by the anaesthetics used, I performed the following experiments:

3) In six cases of birth, the mother was put under chloroform anaesthesia immediately after delivery was complete but before she had seen her lamb. Unconsciousness lasted about half an hour. In all six cases, the mother accepted her lamb without any doubt immediately after she became conscious. Similar experiments with curare gave the same result.

From these and other experiments, I became convinced that without pain, there can be no mother love in nature, and that this pain must actually be experienced psychologically. It is not sufficient for the body to experience it merely physiologically.

Mother love is a *psychological* complex. Therefore, the key which makes it function must be a psychological one, similar to the psychological impression of flight in the case of the termite.

It has been shown what the result of birth pain was in the case of the scorpion mother. In a later chapter, the interesting way in which the same principle is verified in the termite queen will be discussed.

This complex, as we find in all such complexes of the instinctive soul, has long ago ceased functioning in the human. Birth pain has become psychologically a useless rudimentary manifestation, and is now is a source of danger, like most rudimentary organs.

One expert has written:

> "When nature wishes to annihilate a race, the first attack made is in the direction of the sexual sense."

This is a confusing statement, and I am not sure whether it is true. One fact is clear though; that the degeneration of the sexual sense is responsible for the greatest part of human suffering. Yet one aspect of sex – maternal love – has given a twist to humanity's psychological development which has been largely responsible for our domination of the planet.

REALLY?

11
Uninherited Instincts

IT HAS BEEN STATED that in the termite queen, pain accompanies the laying of the first eggs. It is usually very difficult to be certain of the perception of pain in the animal world. The outward signs vary enormously in different species and in varying circumstances.

In general, however, it may be said that the outward signs of pain are more or less similar in all higher animals. If an animal is affected by convulsive spasms, makes needless movements of its limbs, draws back the head, and at the same time moans and groans, it is recognizable that it is in pain. It is not possible, though, to determine the cause of the pain. This expression of pain is an international language amongst animals, and even humans know it from childhood.

Most insects speak the same language, without, however, making audible sounds. Therefore, anyone watching the bodily movements of the queen termite which I have described will feel certain they are an expression of pain.

If one is in any doubt, one can dispel this by actually hurting the queen and comparing her behaviour with that which occurs when she is laying her first eggs. If you touch certain parts of her body with a glass rod dipped in sulphuric acid, an observer will see the identical waving of the antennae, the writhing of the body, and so on. This is exactly what happens when she is laying her eggs.

The greatest proof was found in her behaviour after her eggs were laid. It is not 'scientific' proof of course. I am trying to establish the connection between the cause and effect, and now I am taking the effect as proof of the cause. Yet everyone will grant that a general knowledge of animal behaviour can find proof in itself. As soon as I observed the bodily movements of the queen, I immediately realized that she was in pain. I was then in a position to predict that as result of this, she would, in all probability, show signs of affection for her young. While both occurrences were improbable, it did indicate that the knowledge I possessed could, if necessary, produce proof. Even prior to my studies of the queen, I had come to the conclusion that birth pain was the key to mother love. The following is an account of her behaviour immediately afterwards.

> On the little garden patch where the first eggs are laid, we see the king and queen continually wandering around. They are busy irrigating and fertilizing the fungi beds. Soon, the first larvae appear. We see them wriggling in the garden – small, white, helpless babies, but we can already distinguish the different kinds, the so-called soldiers and the mandibulated (i.e having mouth parts), workers. The queen appears among them. We see something glisten in her jaws. In the stream of light, it looks transparent and as pure as a diamond. Under the magnifying glass, we see that it is a drop of fluid. She approaches one baby after another, they lift their heads and you see the drop disappear. The queen is busy feeding her little ones.

As has been stated, behaviour such as this is unknown in insects at the same stage of development. The nearest approach to anything similar is the observation of von Buttel-Reepen, that a certain bee, *Halictus*, lays her eggs so slowly that the first eggs hatch before she has laid the last, and that she therefore comes into contact with her own living young. It is my belief that in that case, it is sheer chance. It is worth noting that this instance is so exceptional that attention must be paid to it. Of care and feeding, however, there is no mention.

With this feeding and preparation of the first soldiers and workers, the individual labour of the king and queen comes to an end. This signals that the opportunity for observation is finished as well.

From now on, the community suffers from photophobia – fear of light – to such an extent that the usual methods of observation are impossible. This in turn creates focus on a phenomenon which is as mysterious as the transference of the queen from cell to cell. The king and queen do not possess this instinctive photophobia. They are ordinary winged insects, and only a short while before, we saw them in the sunlight, flying around. The soldiers and workers, on the contrary, are totally blind and hate the light. How can they possibly inherit a hereditary instinct which the parents do not possess?

Nor is this all. The soldiers and workers inherit many instincts which the parents do not possess. They begin immediately building complicated structures. They make cells, passages, aqueducts, and a crust, all containing various forms of arch. One can separate a part of the termitary with a steel plate, in such a way that there is no communication between the termites on each side of it. Nevertheless, the same curve of arch, or a lower one, as the case may be, is built on either side of the plate.

They become aware of the presence or absence of light on the surface, through about twelve inches of opaque earth. The termites manufacture cardboard from grass-stalks and wood. They steal eggs from other termites, carry them to the breeding chambers, and care for them. The soldiers and workers take care of the larvae and feed them, but this is of course an instinct which the queen possesses. They make gardens and replant dried-up gardens. From whom do they inherit these hereditary instincts? All soldiers and workers have the same instincts. Throughout nature, we find hereditary instincts of the kind inherited by an organism only from parents with similar instincts.

It is challenging to ask where the special instincts of the sexless forms in the community came from. The king and queen cannot hand them on, because they themselves do not possess them, nor do they take part in, or come in contact with, the communal life of their citizens. Likewise, the soldiers and workers cannot hand on their instincts to other soldiers and workers, for they take no part in the reproduction of the race.

It is interesting to admit that all this had never seemed a mystery to me, for I felt I had long ago discovered the secret. When one knows the answer to a problem, it can never appear impossible to solve!

In some ways, this is the most mysterious occurrence in the life history of the termite. As such, it deserves careful attention. The interesting fact remains that inexperienced observers seldom become aware of these mysteries, let alone have the inclination to find an explanation.

In connection with this riddle, I wanted to show how other European researchers handle cases of this kind, and the explanations they offer. I was able to do this through a correspondent, personally unknown to me, who sent me a monograph written by Professor Dr Bugnion of the University of Lausanne. Dr Bugnion had studied termites in Ceylon for some years, and this monograph was to form part of a monumental work of the famous psychologist Auguste Forel. The title is *The Community World of the Termite*.

Dr Bugnion discussed in particular the wars between the ants and the termites, with special reference to the origin of instinct. As would be the case in any tropical country, Dr Bugnion saw many instances of attacks on termites by ants. He attributes all the instincts and the variations in form of the termites to this continuous state of warfare. In my own research, I saw little evidence of this ant warfare in

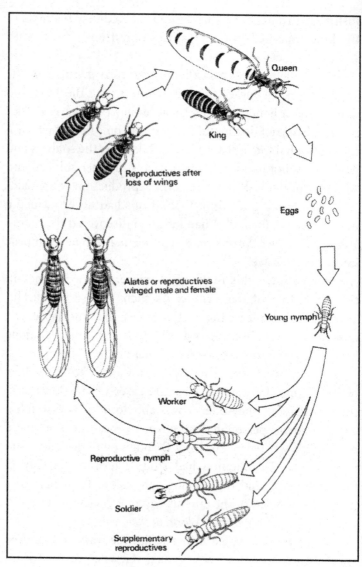

Queen

King

Reproductives after
loss of wings

Eggs

Alates or reproductives
winged male and female

Young nymph

Worker

Reproductive nymph

Soldier

Supplementary
reproductives

The life cycle of termites

Waterberg. On the contrary, our research has shown that one of the nimblest, most ferocious of our flesh-eating ants lives by choice in a termitary belonging to one of the most helpless of termites which possesses no soldier class. If we break open such a termitary, it is easy to get an impression of war. This is nevertheless based on inaccurate observation. There is no war as such; in fact, most probably this behaviour is protection and friendship. This may also be proved by other researchers in the field.

If we break down a number of the smaller termitaries, sooner or later, we come upon one which ants and termites occupy together. Of this small, pale termite there is only one class, the worker. If you look at them under a magnifying glass, it will be evident that their manner of building is entirely different from that of the termites previously studied. The workers immediately appear at the edge of the wound, yet they do not carry stones and stick these together to mend the breach. These pale termites build only with clay. Each worker who appears at the margin of the wound tests a place with its jaws, swings round with a characteristic movement and deposits a small layer of clean, soft mud. Sometimes the worker deposits just a spot, although more frequently it is a little layer. Dr Bugnion had the opportunity to see the collection of this mud, but he could not actually see what the termites were doing. The account that has been given will allow everyone to recognize this particular termite.

Among the termitaries broken into, a section that is inhabited by a dark grey ant – nimble, ferocious and excited – will be found. At first sight, it appears very much as though these ants are determined to slaughter the termites. The dark grey ants run rapidly between and over the termites, appearing to attack with terror and fury. Occasionally, one of them will seize a termite and carry it a short distance. Sometimes a termite will grip the leg of an ant and be dragged about, without apparently causing the ant any harm. The wounded termites are also seized and dragged about. In the meantime, the other termites quite peacefully go about their business of repairing their fortifications. The ants continually touch and test the repairs, but they never attempt to throng into the passages or to hinder the workers in any way. They appear to have special entrances to the innermost parts of the nest.

The observer quickly comes to the conclusion that there is here nothing comparable to murder or war. What it actually was, I had no opportunity of discovering. Much time is necessary to study even a single phenomenon of termite behaviour in a dry country like South Africa. I believe this communal life of termite and ant, whatever its basis may be, holds many surprises in store for scientists. We find, however, in South Africa little evidence of the tropical strife of which Dr Bugnion speaks, and realize that it is extremely easy to come to unsound conclusions.

*

In a later chapter I will try to interpret the first labours of the king and queen. At present it is sufficient to say that with the attainment of adult stature by the workers and soldiers, systematic observation becomes impossible. The first and most important reason for this is the photophobia already mentioned. All the first efforts of the workers and soldiers are concentrated on sealing up all holes by which light can enter, allowing the observer to watch them. If one perseveres and reopens these holes, the termites simply vanish and that is the end of the nest which took so much time and patience to bring into being. It is possible, however, by breaking into many termitaries to form a fairly accurate picture in our minds of the further course of events in the community.

A cement chamber is made for the queen and she is imprisoned there. Passages are made in all directions for the conveyance of coarse food to the different digestive centres; gardens are cultivated on a large scale and planted with

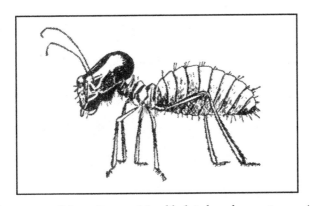

Eutermes or Trinervitermes. Mandibulated worker; water carrier, mason, probably also gardener, nurse and feeder. One of its most important functions is to bring all coarse foodstuff into the general metabolism. These workers form part of what corresponds to the bloodstream in higher animals. Colour: Somewhat etiolated with light red markings. Blind, no organs of hearing, sexless.

fungi; construction of the superficial defensive crust forms an important part of the work.

To come back to this great mystery of inherited instinct, every organism, except the apes and man, inherits from its parents all the instincts – that is, hereditary environmental memory – which it needs for its own struggle for existence. It is born with the knowledge of what kind of food it needs, where and how to obtain it; it knows its natural enemies and how to defend itself against them; it knows how to make a nest or other home; how to feed its little ones and to care for them. All this knowledge is there without the organism having to learn it, without even coming into contact with the other individuals of its race.

I gave an interesting example of this in the South African yellow weaver bird, which, after being kept out of its natural environment for four generations, by hatching the eggs under canaries, instinctively knew how to build its characteristic nest and how to feed its young. No one taught these birds. Four generations of their ancestors had never seen a plaited nest or

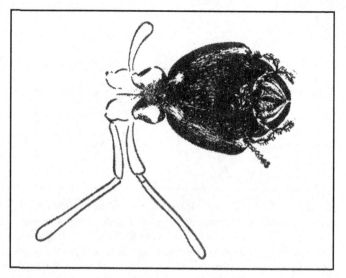

Head of Eutermes worker from below, showing the mouth parts. These are specially developed for purposes of building and feeding.

tasted a worm, yet the fifth generation knew what to do.

This is what is called instinct, or hereditary environmental memory.

In the termite we find three apparently different insects – the queens, the workers and the soldiers, being produced from one father and mother who are completely different from two of the forms that their offspring take. If one did not actually know the contrary, one would believe the inmates of the termitary to be completely different insects.

With the physical difference go special hereditary memories or instincts. The soldier is armed with the first hypodermic syringe made by Nature, which she eventually perfected in the poison fangs of the adder. In his polished head the termite soldier carries a little flask of poison and on his forehead a needle-like tube through which the sticky fluid is squirted. It uses this weapon only against threatening enemies or strangers.

The worker has strong, well-made jaws and a glue-producing gland which it uses in its complicated building operations.

As soon as it has reached adult status the worker begins to make gardens, care for and feed the king and queen, tend the hatching eggs, carry food, and partially digest it for the benefit of the whole community.

Both these insects are totally blind, neither of them possesses eyes or other organs of sense; nevertheless they are aware of the presence or absence of light through twenty-four inches of compact earth.

12

The Mysterious Power which Governs

THE TERMITES DIG DEEP BOREHOLES to find water, and from this source it is conveyed for general purposes. When a breach is made in a termitary, the syringe-bearing soldiers are the first to appear. They inspect the damage slowly and thoughtfully from all sides. If there are no workers at hand, or only a few, the soldiers begin to signal. By quick movements of the throat plates of their armour, they make a *tik-tik-tik* sound. In houses infested by termites, this sound can be heard at night in all directions. With this signal the soldiers summon the workers to the place of attack. The same sound is used as a food signal. So urgent is this call that even workers who have been appointed to special tasks, like conveying water, carrying the larvae, gardening, and feeding of the royal pair drop their work and rush to the place from where the alarm has sounded.

As I have shown before, the behaviour of the two kinds of termite corresponds in every respect to the functions of the blood corpuscles in higher animals. Just as the white corpuscles make a cordon round the wound, which the red corpuscles begin healing, the soldiers form a protective circle while the workers repair the breach. If you annoy the soldiers individually, with a sharp object like a needle, they go into a kind of convulsion. Their bodies jerk angrily from side to

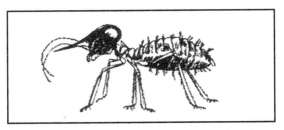

Eutermes nasicorn soldier, with syringe. Blind, deaf, sexless. Colour: Head, reddish-yellow; body, blood red. Generally highly pigmented. Mouth parts, rudimentary. Function: 1. Part of the 'blood-stream'. 2. Defence, when outer layer of termitary is attacked.

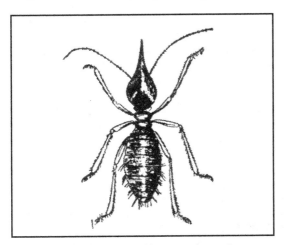

Eutermes nasicorn soldier seen from above.

side and through their syringe-like weapon they squirt a drop of clear sticky fluid in the direction of the danger. This fluid appears to cause extreme pain to other small insects, glues together their jaws and legs, and renders them helpless.

All these actions are instinctive. It is worthwhile revisiting the question: where do the termites get these instincts?

That their behaviour must be inherited cannot be doubted, because all the workers and soldiers possess exactly the same instincts as the others of their type. It is impossible for them to have inherited these from their father and mother, because neither the king nor the queen possesses any of these instincts. The royal pair possess perfect eyes and do not fear the light as the workers and soldiers do. On the other hand, they do not possess a special, but inexplicable sense which enables them to perceive the dimmest ray of light as their offspring do. They know nothing of collective building of termitaries, of squirting poison, or carrying water. They do not even come in touch with the labours of the community.

It would appear that we are forced to come to the conclusion that the workers and soldiers inherit a large number of environmental memories which neither of their parents ever possessed. On the other hand, they do *not* inherit some of the characteristics of their father and mother, for they cannot fly, never copulate and never lay eggs. They themselves cannot hand on their instincts to other soldiers and workers, for they never produce young. It appears to be a paradox.

It is also interesting to note the observations of Dr Bugnion of Ceylon, and how he explained the mystery. I will quote what he says about his difficulties, discuss his theories, and then give my own criticism of them.

He says:

> "When the biologist, having satisfied himself that (1) the soldiers who are trusted with the task of defence are totally blind, and that (2) the workers who do the repairs are small, insignificant insects, not more than five millimetres in length, and when he sees the collective drive of the termites, he becomes perplexed and amazed. His wonder increases when he tries to discover the power that governs the termites and the moral law which binds them together – and finds no trace of it."

It is difficult to understand exactly what Dr Bugnion means. I think what he meant to say was:

> 'The biologist clearly sees the effects of a governing power and a moral bond.'

What the biologist does not discover so easily is the source of this governing power and moral bond. Dr Bugnion continues:

> "Finally, the biologist is forced to conclude that the activity of these little insects, which appear to behave so intelligently and thoughtfully, is entirely instinctive."

I must admit that intelligence and thoughtfulness, as we humans understand these qualities, never entered my mind in connection with the termites. Perhaps I was lucky enough to discover the secret of the behaviour of the termites too soon for those considerations. It is also possible that perhaps I knew just sufficient about behaviourism in animals to prevent me from going too far astray. I know it is extremely easy to be sidetracked in studies of comparative psychology, when there has been little opportunity to learn about animals in their natural surroundings and when human intelligence is used as the criterion of judgement.

In describing the wonderful collective activity of the workers and soldiers, Dr Bugnion stated:

> "It is amazing how they can do all this without a single mistake."

He is wrong, however, for they make many mistakes. They often go to work mistakenly and persevere in their mistakes. Remember the useless turrets in this respect, excrescences which form a danger to the community. As clever as they are in one direction, they are unbelievably stupid in other directions. On the other hand, Dr Bugnion must have missed perceiving the real building genius which the termite possesses, or else he would not have risked giving such a confident explanation. The solution given above, of course, is not very convincing. To say that the work of the termites is instinctive is like trying to explain the nature of wind by saying it is wind. The actual problem confronting us is not whether the activity of the termites is governed by reason or instinct, but who is the architect who designs the plans which the workers execute?

If we look at the workers through a magnifying glass, you can see them appear one by one from the dark depths, each carrying a tiny grain of earth. Without the least thought, each worker rolls the pebble round and round in its jaws. It covers it with a sticky mucilage, sets it in position in the breach and vanishes again into the depths. You cannot imagine for one moment that every small worker is conscious of the purpose of its work, or that it carries in its mind the plan, or even part of the plan, of the building operations. The tower or breach may be a million times larger than the termite itself. The workers attack the repairs from every side, and are totally blind. We can see that the termites at one side of the breach never come into contact with those on the other side. They may fetch their materials from different parts of the nest.

If we have any doubt of this we can easily dispel it. Take a steel plate a few feet wider and higher than the termitary. Drive it right through the centre of the breach you have made, in such a way that you divide the wound and the termitary into two separate parts. One section of the community can never be in touch with the other, and one of the sections will be separated from the queen's cell. The builders on one side of the breach know nothing of those on the other side. In spite of this the termites build a similar arch or tower on each side of the plate. When eventually you withdraw the plate, the two halves match perfectly after the dividing cut has been repaired.

We cannot escape the conclusion that somewhere there exists a preconceived plan which the termites execute. Where is the soul, the psyche, in which this preconception exists? That is the problem which must be solved. Dr Bugnion says it is instinct. If we accept that, then *whose* instinct? Does he maintain that every tiny worker carries part of the plan in its little soul? The experiment with the steel plate disposes of this theory. Even if one could prove that every worker had an instinctive knowledge of part of the plan, then the ultimate problem would still remain unsolved.

Where does each worker obtain his part of the general design? We can drive in the steel plate first and *then* make a breach on either side, and still the termites build identical structures on each side. It cannot be an inherited tendency, for the termites do not always build the same kind of arch or other structure. We can find a dozen different widths of arch near the surface of a large termitary. These arches are one of the amazing features of the termites' building powers.

It cannot be due to the instinctive knowledge of the individual termite. If the termite always built one kind of form, one kind of tower, one kind of arch, we might perhaps come to the conclusion that it worked according to instinctive or inherited knowledge. Even then a doubt would exist. We are inclined to imagine the termites think and reason in a way similar to our own mental processes. Yet we know that they possess perceptive powers a million times more acute than our own senses. They become aware, for instance, from a fleeting touch of another termite, that it belongs to their own nest. They then follow its trail towards food, with unfailing certainty. From this has arisen the theory of 'intelligent communication' which Dr Bugnion and even Forel still appear to subscribe to. By touch, they can perceive alarm and agitation in a fellow termite, and can apparently tell where the danger lies. They become aware over incredible distances of the signals of the soldiers; all these things they sense without a vestige of a sense organ.

How can one compare this soul with that of a human being? When one sees a tiny worker termite placing a single grain of sand which will eventually become part of a massive tower twelve or fifteen feet high, millions upon millions of times larger than itself, can you assume for one moment that the worker knows, in the human sense, what the final result of its work is going to be? If this were so, its intelligence would be that of a god, compared with our own.

His work is naturally due to instinct, as Dr Bugnion says, but it is not the instinct of the individual worker. It is the instinct and design of a separate soul, situated outside the individual termite.

If we carry our recent experiment a little further, new light begins to be shed on our problem.

While the termites are carrying on their work of restoration on either side of the steel plate, dig a furrow enabling you to reach the queen's cell, disturbing the nest as little as possible. Expose the queen and destroy her. Immediately, the whole community ceases work on either side of the plate. We can separate the termites from the queen for months by means of this plate, yet in spite of that, they continue working systematically while she is alive in her cell; destroy or remove her, however, and their activity ceases immediately.

If the termitary under observation is in the neighbourhood of other termitaries, we can establish a few more facts experimentally. If there is a termitary within a yard or two, one can prove that the termites of both nests mix freely without fighting. Place a piece of wood equidistant from both nests and spray the ground around it with water. If you expose the passages, you will soon find that termites from both nests are destroying the wood. If you break into these two termitaries and put workers and soldiers from one nest into the other, you will find they do not get attacked. If, however, you do the same to termitaries that are twenty or thirty yards from each other, then the strangers are pounced on immediately by workers and soldiers, and killed.

If you destroy the queen in one of the two nests that are very close each other, then the termites of that nest cease work and move to the adjoining nest where they apparently swear allegiance to the new queen. If, however, you destroy the queen of a nest which is some distance from another, the termites make no attempt to transfer to another nest, but die in their old home. The reason for this difference in conduct would appear to be that the mysterious power which streams from the queen functions only within a limited distance. Every termite is under the influence of this power. If their two termitaries are situated close to each other, the power of each queen operates in both nests. It is through this psychological power of the queen that the termites of one nest are capable of recognizing their fellow termites and discovering strange intruders.

The following experiment shows this clearly.

Take soldiers and workers from one nest and place them in a far distant nest and make certain that they really are attacked, by waiting until the disturbance caused by the breach has died down; then destroy the queen of the first nest. If you transfer termites as before, immediately after you have killed the queen, you will find they are again attacked. If, however, you wait a day or two and *then* transfer the termites, they are no longer attacked, but are accepted as new members of the community.

It appears therefore, as if the workers and soldiers carry with them *something* of their own queen. We will assume it is something similar to scent, although I think it is something much more subtle. But if we think of it as scent, it will simplify matters, even though we are actually dealing with something far beyond the human senses.

The power of the queen reaches only certain fixed limits. It can penetrate earth, rock and even metal plates. It evaporates within one or two days. It is the mainspring of all the collective activity of the soldiers and workers. The queen is the psychological centre of the community; she is the brain of the organism which we call a termitary.

From this shapeless, immobile object, imprisoned in her narrow vault, there emanates a power which directs all the activities of her subjects. This is how our own brain rules the functions of the blood corpuscles, and regulates and keeps in order the composite animal we call our body.

Dr Bugnion did not discover the psychological functions

of the queen. He assumed that the king and queen possess only sexual functions. He accordingly encountered all kinds of inexplicable difficulties which I did not face.

If only Dr Bugnion had had the opportunity to accompany a professional South African termite-catcher, he would, without any doubt, have discovered the secret. I was fortunate enough to have had this chance. His greatest difficulty was the problem of where the soldiers and workers get their hereditary memory. He found two solutions. The first was founded on the fact that some observers discovered individuals of the sexless forms possessing perfect organs. He assumed, therefore, that the sexless forms were at one time fertile. Then he says:

> "Given these facts, we have only to conceive of the period during which the defence methods were perfected as coinciding with the period during which the workers and soldiers were fertile in order to render more plausible the hereditary transmission of the improvements in question and of the instincts (neoform) related to them."

If this is so, he must accept the theory that the present queen and king types are descended from the present sexless types. That cannot be true, as actually the very opposite is the case. I do not think any one can fail to accept the theory that the termite was originally a single flying insect of the same type as the present king and queen. The founding of community life was the cause of the physical differentiation into workers and soldiers. With these changes, new instincts arose. The laying of eggs by workers is a very rare occurrence. You can also occasionally find rudimentary eyes and wing-buds in a few soldiers. These are all atavisms, which show that the original termite was a fertile flying insect. One thing is certain – both the changed physical characteristics and the new instincts are transmitted by the queen, although she does not possess, nor did she ever possess, either of these things herself.

There is another fact which Dr Bugnion has not touched

on. How does it happen that the soldiers and workers not only inherit instincts which their father and mother did not possess, but they also do *not* inherit the specialized instincts that the father and mother *do* possess?

The second explanation which Dr Bugnion puts forward is somewhat surprising. He must have been quite confused when he wrote the following:

> "As the workers and soldiers live in the interior of the compartments in the company of the sexual forms until the moment of swarming, it is not entirely incredible, judging by the above suggestion (that the ants and termites carry on intelligent communication with each other), that while they are living together they should exchange a few ideas. As a result of these communications new instincts acquired by the workers and soldiers would become the property of the community as a whole."

If Dr Bugnion had said that he had seen a termite soldier giving birth to a whale it could not have sounded more 'entirely incredible' than the above statement! The workers and soldiers are supposed to tell their work and plans to the queen; she remembers what she is told, and conveys this knowledge to the workers and soldiers she gives birth to later.

Dr Bugnion maintained his belief in the 'intelligent communication' of ants and termites. He called it 'antennae-language'.

There is only one conclusion which corresponds properly with all our knowledge of termite behaviour. The individual worker or soldier possesses no *individual* instincts. It forms part of a separate and composite organism, of which the queen is the psychological centre. The queen has the power – call it *instinct* – of influencing the soldiers and workers in a certain way, which enables them to perform collective duties. This power or instinct is transmitted to all queens born from her. As soon as the queen is destroyed, all the instincts of workers and soldiers immediately cease. She transmits this psychological power to the future queens, just as she transmits to them the power of producing three infinitely different forms of insect: the queen, the worker and the soldier.

At times, Dr Bugnion comes very close to discovering the secret. He says:

> "The multifarious duties which are carried out under our eyes by the soldiers on the one hand and the workers on the other give us the illusion of a higher direction, whereas in reality this direction does not exist, or if it does exist, resides solely in the community as a whole."

Later he says:

> "The male and female individuals which are described in the higher termites as king and queen have no authority and possess no power of any kind. The king and queen termite shut in their closed cell do not even know what is happening outside. It would be impossible for them to give orders from the depths of their prison.'

One notices that Dr Bugnion constantly talks of the termites as if they have human understanding: "to know and to give orders".

He thinks anthropomorphically all the time. He assumes that the termites are able to 'talk', but that touch is necessary for this. He never considers a subtle, immaterial influence which functions at a distance. He should have asked the question: "How does the queen hold the community together from her cell in the depths?"

There are millions of her subjects which never come into contact with her, and which have never seen her. Yet, as soon as she is destroyed, there is an immediate end to the community as such. Our 'ant-catchers' here in the Transvaal never attempt to destroy directly the millions of workers and soldiers in the nest; instead they take out the queen. For every queen, they receive a fee of two pounds. Dr Bugnion, and every observer, must be aware of this sustaining power of the queen, and also realize that she has functions other than merely sexual. The queen has some psychological function which neither depth nor imprisonment can frustrate. From this realization, it is only a single step further to the discovery of all her psychological functions. Similarly, it might also be asked: How can an organ like the brain, which is shut up in a vault, direct and know the functions of the blood corpuscles, even in the toes?

One more word about the origin of the instinct of the termites. Dr Bugnion says:

> "The origin of most of these instincts is a reasoned and conscious action."

I find it difficult to believe that this explanation could be made seriously today. What would Dr Bugnion say of hundreds of our South African desert plants, which have so cleverly adapted to their environment? Have these plants also reasoned and thought in human fashion, thus solving one difficulty after another, and transmitted this knowledge to their descendants?

All this discussion has been caused by the wonderful change which has taken place in the termitary from the time when we saw the queen feeding her young ones and when a few months later we open the palace cell for observation. These changes are an amazing discovery for a psychologist.

In the first instance, we were observing an ordinary flying insect at work, behaving in a normal manner with normal reactions – except of course, the birth pain and mother-love reactions. In our later observations, a new soul and a new body have appeared. The queen is no longer the insect she was. She has received a new soul.

What has she become? How can one classify her? It is difficult to find a place for her in a classified list. A biologist may consider placing her with the soldiers and workers. The psychologist would counteract by saying that these are also not insects in the normal sense of the word. Psychologists classify all living organisms according to their behaviour. The workers and soldiers, with only the merest semblance of an individual psyche, fall outside all classes.

It is unnecessary to suppose that the termites are capable of talking, thinking, acting and remembering in a human fashion. In most instances, an observer seeks to find the simplest explanation first, yet Dr Bugnion's example shows us that this is not always the case. His two theories are based on the hypothesis that the termites are simply small humans for whom 'an exchange of ideas' is possible. According to Bugnion, the queen, before her flight, walks round the nest, and comes into contact with the workers and soldiers. She studies their community life, and there is 'an exchange of ideas'.

From this point, Dr Bugnion becomes even more difficult to understand. What he appears to mean is that the queen remembers the lessons she learnt from the workers and soldiers, although she never herself takes part in their labours. Similarly, she herself never shows any signs of the specialized instinct which animates the workers and soldiers, yet in spite of this, she transmits these lessons to her offspring. According to Dr Bugnion, the queen does something which humans have not succeeded in doing. Humans do not transmit a single acquired memory to their offspring; the son of the greatest mathematician does not inherit even the multiplication table.

There is not a single fact or condition in nature or in the life history of the termite which justifies Dr Bugnion's opinion. His theories seem to have been pure speculation. There is one great difficulty which Dr Bugnion obviously did not notice, as he does not mention it. Suppose his theory is right – that the queen transmits the special instincts to her offspring in this way. There still remains the problem of how the queen manages to give birth to two kinds of insect which resemble her as little as a scorpion does a butterfly. This cannot be due to the lessons she 'learnt' from the soldiers and workers in the original termitary. Why does she transmit the special instincts to only two kinds of young, which do not inherit her own instincts, while she does not transmit these acquired instincts to the third type of her offspring, the potential queens? The future queens inherit not only her own physical form, but also all her special instincts, and not a single one of the instincts of the soldiers and workers. His theory cannot be correct.

His other theory is that the soldiers and workers were at one time fertile, and that the present types are the descendants of those soldier and worker ancestors. This assumption means that the difficulty of explaining how the queen manages to divide her inherited memories, some of which are latent, among her three types of offspring remains.

I will compare all this with my own theory. I believe that the termite was originally a single flying insect, exposed to all kinds of dangers. To keep her eggs and offspring safe, she took refuge in an underground shelter. Here, just as happens with the bee, *Halictus*, she came into contact with her young after they were hatched. This was the beginning of community life.

Finally, to cause the community to function well, there was a division of labour. Some of the insects had to build and look for food, while others had to protect the nest. Compare the story of *Siphonophora*, already mentioned. The queen who tended to produce offspring more suitable for the various kinds of labour would have a greater chance of survival than one who did not have this tendency, and so natural selection began to operate. The present-day soldiers and workers were the fittest types for protection and building operations, and the sexual types for reproduction. The queen who had the tendency to produce these three types had more chance of survival, and transmitted this tendency to the females born from her.

Natural selection thus operated in two directions. The nearer the workers and soldiers came physically to the present-day types, the more chance the community had of surviving.

A queen was selected naturally, therefore, who gave birth to all three types. Finally, a queen and king were selected who not only produced these three types, but who possessed the psychological power to influence the community and to take the place of the individual instincts of the workers and soldiers.

It is easy to understand why it was an advantage to the community for the sexual sense to be destroyed in all types. Even the sexual types (potential kings and queens), possess no sexuality while they remain in the termitary. Sex in such a community would have been a disturbing influence which would have suspended all protective and other work over long periods. In order to carry out the best labour, the workers and the soldiers had to become mere automata, governed by the psychological power of the queen. For the same reason, they lost their sight and other senses, which are the accompaniment of an individual psyche.

The soldiers and workers, therefore, do not inherit any special instincts from their parents. It is the queen who inherits the power of transmitting the semblance of such instincts to the automatons who work for her.

13
The Water Supply

IN MANY PARTS OF THE WORLD we find people studying the life history of termites. In spite of this, no single observer seems to have discovered the psychological functions of the queen, and more surprising still, no one seems to have realized the intriguing mystery of the constant supply of water of the termitary.

Barthellier, a Frenchman, has studied the termite in Indo-China, in districts probably as dry as Waterberg. An Englishman, Carpenter, studied certain termites for a long time in British East Africa; Maxwell Le Roy in India; Prell, a German, in German East Africa; the Belgians Hegh and Ghesguière in the Congo; Hill in Australia; and many others in parts of North and South America. The collected works of all these observers and many others would fill a library. Yet none of them ever sought to answer the questions:

1) Why does the community life of soldiers and workers cease when the queen is destroyed?

2) Where do the termites get their water?

These facts seem to have escaped their notice; that is, the never-ceasing supply of water during the driest seasons, and the change of behaviour caused by the destruction of the queen. If these things are not observed, then of course, the problems and unavoidable investigation of them will not arise.

I want to describe my own observations of the conveyance

of water. I was very impressed at the time by the result of my observations and also the effect they had on the other spectators. The behaviour of these people was as interesting as the behaviour of the termites. It was sheer chance which gave me the opportunity of watching for months the terrific struggle – and it was very much a struggle between life and death – and it unfolded like a film on the screen.

It was during the most severe drought which had ever stricken the Waterberg. None had occurred like this within human memory. On the farm *Reitfontein 1638*, where my observations took place, a sixty-year-old orange grove was entirely destroyed by the drought. There were many signs that it was the peak of a period of drought which had been gradually, but systematically increasing, for over 300 years.

Just behind the farmhouse on *Rietfontein* was a range of hills which divided the farm in half. On the brow of the range were innumerable castles of the Waterberg termite. Many of these termitaries had been dead for some time, but equally as many were, even during the very worst of the drought, still alive and intact. I had often wondered about their secret water supply, but at this time it became a bewildering puzzle to me. The whole atmosphere was so dry that even at night there was not the least semblance of dew.

The whole surface of the farm was intersected with canals and ditches, and it could be confirmed by careful examination that along the range there was no trace of water in the earth to a depth of 40 feet. As a result of extremely hard labour, we opened two termitaries situated on the summit of the hills. In one we found an eight foot cobra, which covered old Mr Gys van Rooyen and myself with venom. Both of us received it full in the face, but luckily our eyes escaped. (The 'ringhals', or ringneck, of the Boers, *Naja nigricollis*, has the power of spitting its venom to a range of about six feet. It aims at the eyes, and is very accurate.)

In both these termitaries, the palace cavity was six feet

Termite runways on a tree

below the surface of earth that was as hard as rock. Yet the whole of the palace cavity and the fungus gardens were moist. In the palace cavity, the temperature was two degrees above the normal blood temperature of a human. Water vapour was present in all the passages. The queen and all her subjects appeared to be perfectly normal.

The only unusual feature we found was that many of the gardens near the palace had dried up. Where did the termites obtain their water? I came eventually to the conclusion that the termites, in some way or other, manufactured water from oxygen and hydrogen. Where they obtained the hydrogen was another inexplicable mystery. However, I knew the termites were capable of many wonderful things, and at the time my solution seemed the only possible one.

I first came close to the truth through an account given to me by Mr Jan Wessel Wessels, an outstanding practical naturalist. He told me that while he was living in Bechuanaland (Botswana), he had twice observed in wells vertical canals made by the termites, descending to incredible depths in order to reach water.

I still felt though, that this solution was difficult to accept. The termites on the range at Rietfontein would have had to go down vertically to a depth of at least a hundred feet to obtain water.

Then again, all our attempts at finding the beginning of such an aqueduct were unsuccessful. Later, we discovered the reason for this. It was only the widely known and undoubted trustworthiness of Mr Wessels which allowed me to accept this explanation. Then, as a result of mere chance, I too was able to see the whole system functioning.

In this terrible drought, it was not only the termites who were seeking water, but humans as well. On the brow of the range, a clump of green bushes contrasted starkly with the parched *veld*. Mr Van Rooyen thought there must be water at this spot, and his belief was confirmed by a water diviner. Excavation immediately began of a square pit in the centre of the green clump. When the pit was about forty feet deep, I was told by the labourers that a termite runway was visible on the north wall, for its whole depth. I lost no time in going to the spot to study the amazing work in detail.

The first fact I established was that the termitary connected with this canal was at least thirty feet away from the pit. I exposed the whole tunnel, and also, part of the gardens adjacent to the palace cavity. The latter I covered with a wooden lid, to enable me to observe them from time to time. I then discovered that the aqueduct did not descend vertically from the nest, but from the end of a long horizontal passage. This was the reason for our failing to discover it in the termitaries we opened.

I was then able to discern a fact in relation to termite behaviour which would have helped me to infer the existence of a shaft into the depths, before actually seeing one, by allowing me to reason more clearly.

When the ground is wet, in rainy seasons, the workers always begin repairing any damage to the outer crust immediately. In dry seasons, however, it takes hours, sometimes days, before the builders make their appearance and tackle the work. No wonder, if each little worker has to descend hundreds of feet to get its masonry. However, this solution initially escaped me. I simply did not think of it!

Another noteworthy point in connection with the vertical shaft was that in one plane – north/south – there were absolutely no bends. In the other plane – east/west – there were many unnecessary bends. This meant that the shaft was visible through its whole length on the north wall of the well, in spite of the turnings east and west. The vertical direction in one plane was of course a great labour-saving to the termites; but why did they not make the borehole absolutely vertical? Their method, like everything else they do, appeared almost, but not absolutely, perfect. They are extremely wise in some ways and yet very stupid in others.

It is possible that the magnetic poles of the earth may have had an influence on this work of the termites. In Australia, there is a certain termite, the Magnetic White Ant, which builds an elongated termitary, with the longer axis pointing north and south. In their case there is no doubt that their building is determined by the magnetic poles of the Earth. So remarkable are the bends occurring only in one plane in the aqueduct of the termites that it is feasible to accept the theory that the perpendicularity in one plane is due to the magnetism of the earth. East and West, however, there is no magnetic power to keep the termites in the vertical direction.

Every two or three feet in the shaft, there was situated a small white garden patch that was dry and unplanted. It should not be forgotten, however, that I probably never saw more than half of the shaft. At a depth of forty feet, the well was abandoned because the ground even there was still as dry as a bone, whereas Mr Van Rooyen and the water diviner had thought a plentiful supply would be found at 25 feet. The distance of the nest from the bottom of the well was 65 feet, and the shaft disappeared into the earth. There is no doubt that there were live gardens deeper down and nearer the water.

I constantly examined under the microscope workers coming up the shaft, and nearly all of them had hyphae, seed ready for planting, in their bodies. Through my observations, I came to these conclusions:

1) That the community could not exist a single day in the terrible drought without water.

2) That this could be the only shaft by which water was conveyed; as even for workers like the termites, it would take years to reach that depth.

3) That they were forced to use this shaft even in its exposed state, in spite of their intense aversion to light.

It was impossible for them to make a new shaft, and there was no chance of covering the old shaft, for haste in the termites' struggle was essential.

In the end, I was proven correct in all my conclusions. It was one of the few times when a prediction was a certainty. I had the opportunity to watch their struggle for existence for months, and to learn about and understand them, step by step. During this time, I visited the shaft at all hours of the day and night, from sunset to sunrise. Not on one of these occasions did I ever observe that their labour ever stopped. In fact, there was not even so much as a pause. I once marked a number of workers with aniline blue and could establish the fact that they never rested or slept. Indeed, they worked day and night, and the same workers who were marked during the day were also busy at night, climbing up and down.

It is noteworthy that in the beginning I did not get the impression of the termites' haste or alarm, which I noticed so clearly some time later. There were two streams of workers; those on the right going down, and those on the left going up. This order was maintained throughout the whole process. The two streams were in single file, with a distance of about two inches separating each termite from the next one. The workers I marked took, in the beginning, about half an hour to reach the end of the shaft and return to the nest with their load from the depths. Later on, this period shortened until it became about twenty minutes.

I then became aware that the whole character of the activity was changing. There was a slowly increasing concentration on the aqueduct. The streams of termites became thicker and thicker, and I got an impression of general alarm. It took me a long time to discover the reason for this. I could see they were occupied with some task which completely taxed the energy and power of resistance of the community. What exactly did it signify?

All repair work totally stopped. No attempt was made to cover over the shaft. A breach made in the termitary was simply ignored, while all the workers and soldiers in the neighbourhood disappeared. After a week or ten days, a limited cordon of soldiers appeared at the edge of the wound, and the workers made occasional attempts at repair. The necessary building materials were brought from the depths of the shaft. I concluded that all the disturbance and heightened circulation was concentrated on the palace cavity, and that the object of it was to convey water to the queen, larvae and soldiers. I knew that the queen was largely a bag of liquid; that she laid on an average 150,000 eggs every 24 hours, and that for the purposes of all her functions, she must require a constant and copious supply of water. Similarly, 90 per cent of the bodies of the rest of the termites consisted of water.

However, the provision of water to the living termites was not the only reason for my heightened interest. When I exposed the outer gardens, I noticed that on a line dividing the gardens in two, there was a constantly crawling throng of termites. I had forgotten that for the king and queen, and for the larvae and soldiers, these gardens were just as necessary as a water supply. The gardens, as I explained before, are digestive organs, without which the community could not exist for even one day.

All the above-mentioned types of termite are entirely dependent on the gardens, for the workers are the only type which can make use of partially digested food. The gardens are the stomach and the liver of the composite animal. The workers are the mouth and teeth.

In order for me to understand what the enormous concentration of effort on the gardens meant, I had to undertake extensive, very careful observation. At last, I noticed that all the gardens that were external to the line were parched, and that this death of the gardens was creeping inward, from day to day. It was on this line dividing the dead gardens from the living that I found the greatest concentration of activity. It took the form of a ferocious attack that did not allow the workers and soldiers a moment's rest. It was a huge struggle against death, and there was no respite for the defenders, day or night.

The workers were engaged in replanting hyphae around the living gardens, and in irrigating these freshly planted seeds. Every little seed and every drop of moisture had to be carried a hundred feet out of the depths of the earth. I could see 65 feet of this distance. During the night, the defenders would gain ground. During this cool period, when evaporation was at its lowest point, the line would be pushed outwards, by a half or a quarter of an inch. Throughout the heat of the day, however, the enemy would press heavily and regain the termite's hard-won advance.

It was during the quietest hours at night that the fierceness of the fight increased in its frenzy. I could distinctly hear the unceasing alarm calls of the soldiers, a sound which aroused, even in me, a feeling of terrible anxiety. My electric searchlight revealed the restless stream constantly passing back and forth; their fate seemed to be inevitable. Nothing could turn them from their purpose, and no external threat could distract them. The death of a thousand individuals made not the least impression on that living stream.

I began to realize the full extent of what the struggle for existence really means in nature.

14

The First Architects

EVERY INVESTIGATOR of termite classification or behaviour must, at one time or another, have been astonished by the ambitious nature of their building and engineering operations. The mightiest structures ever built – the pyramids of Egypt, London's Underground system, New York's skyscrapers, the Simplon tunnel, the biggest cathedrals, the longest bridges – these, compared with works of the termite – taking into consideration its size – are like mole-hills compared with mountains.

Wilhelm Böche, in *Der Termiten Staat*, made some calculations to show how the work of humans compares with that of the termite. Taking size into consideration, humans would have to erect a building as high as the Matterhorn, that is 14,760 feet, if such work was to be equal to a termite tower 40 feet in height, such as is often found in Africa. It is not only the size of the termitary, however, which amazes the investigator, but the almost incredible extent of their underground activity.

I have already described their vertical boreholes, those mighty feats of engineering which they have been forced to carry out in their ceaseless struggle against drought. They are forced to penetrate the bowels of the earth in their constant search for water, which they then have to convey, drop by drop, in order to keep their large communities from death. The actual depth of these shafts is unknown; – exactly how much deeper is uncertain, in addition to the 65 feet previously mentioned.

A tower termitary

The following is an account of some facts which I became aware of when I made a journey through the valley of the Limpopo and the *lowveld* of Zoutpansberg. It was during this journey that I was able to fully grasp and appreciate the astounding genius for building which termites possess.

Everyone who is interested in termites may have read and probably seen photographs of the enormous termitaries which are found in tropical parts of Africa. In the *lowveld* of Zoutpansberg I found some giants, and these were by no means the exception. In some parts of the Limpopo valley, these gigantic termitaries are a very usual feature of the landscape. An engineer, Norman Hugel, carefully measured and calculated the weight of earth making up one colossus structure, and found that it consisted of 11,750 tons of earth. This termitary belonged to a small *Eutermes*. All of the material in the termitary had been piled up grain by grain, for *Eutermes* never uses mud for building purposes; they use only microscopic grains of sand. Every one is rubbed clean and polished before being coated with a sticky cement, then every tiny stone is carefully placed in the right place.

So, grain by grain, the termites heaped up a structure weighing 11,750 tons. You would imagine it would take thousands of years to accomplish, but it was impossible to try to estimate the period of time. There is no doubt that it was a matter of centuries.

There is yet another mystery connected with this particular activity of the termites, which other observers do not seem to have touched on. The puzzle is, from where does the enormous mass of earth come? Researchers would expect to find a hollow cavity below such a vast growth; a hollow in the earth corresponding in size to the superficial mass, because there is no doubt that all the building material is carried from below. However, no signs of any cavity have ever been found, although many of the giant structures have been dissected in many parts of Africa. They have even been totally demolished for purposes of road-making, railway lines, house building, dams, airstrips and all the other constructions of modern civilization.

For instance, in order to level the surface of the Bulawayo airstrip alone, 20,000 tons of 'ant-heap' was carted away. In all such cases, especially when making railways, dams or heavy

A pagoda, or mushroom, termitary

buildings, the ground is always carefully tested for cavities after the surface termitaries have been removed; yet no hollows corresponding in size to the superficial structures have ever been found. Nevertheless, we know that the building material of the termites *must* come out of the earth.

It is important to recall that I discovered the source of the termite water supply by sheer chance. After many years of attempting to solve the problem, I came to the wrong conclusion that the insects manufactured water from hydrogen and oxygen.

If only I had approached the matter in a more reasoned manner, it is possible that these giant termitaries with no cavities below them would have led me to the truth. In the first place, millions of litres of water were necessary to build these structures, plus a further inexhaustible supply for the needs of the termites themselves and the internal functioning of the vast termitary. A quite considerable stream of water must flow into the nest day and night, to keep the community alive.

The explanation now seems to be quite evident: both water and building material come from innumerable tiny cavities in the earth, which the termites are constantly increasing. This is for the purpose of enlarging both the termitary and their water supply as the community grows. It seems to be a cycle.

In another instance, I found a rocky *kopje* or hill in the Sabie Valley which consisted of one vast termitary belonging to the much-feared *Macrotermes bellicosus*, the 'Fighting Termite'. The bite of the bloodthirsty soldiers of *M. bellicosus* goes deep enough to cause considerable bleeding. I took one of these soldiers back to Pretoria and managed to keep it alive for a week after its separation from the nest. The soldier could bite right through the wood of a matchbox with a crunch that could be heard clearly at a distance of four or five yards.

This termitary, consisting of a whole *kopje*, created even more questions for me to consider in my research. I could not accept the idea that the huge rocks on its summit had been heaved up by the building operations of the termites. It is true that Dr Preller and I found stones weighing ten and twelve kilograms high up in the termitaries of *Eutermes* at Pelindaba, which could only have got there through elevation by the termites. However, on the *kopje* there were rocks that were hundreds of tons in weight. Every inch of ground between and under these rocks consisted of the pebble-built structures of

144

M. bellicosus. The probable solution was that the termites had first removed all the original earth between the rocks and then substituted their own pebble work.

I had never seen anything like this occurring before, and the question of what they had done with all the original earth still remained. There was simply *no* sign of normal earth.

This case provides yet another an illustration of the countless and apparently insoluble problems which constantly confront the researcher.

During this journey, I took the opportunity to conduct some experiments to find out in what way, and to what degree, magnetism affects the termite. Mr Piet Haak of Pretoria lent me a dozen of the strongest steel magnets obtainable. I quickly became convinced, however, that my magnetic field was still too weak. To come to any certain conclusion, a powerful electromagnet would have to be used. I have no doubt, however, that the magnetic force of the earth influences the work of all termites. In this connection, one should remember the water shaft at Waterberg that had bends only east and west.

The 'Compass Termites' of Australia build their termitaries with the narrowest diameter towards magnetic north. Mr Claude Fuller alleged that the summits of the termitaries of *M. bellicosus* always lean towards the true west.

In the *lowveld*, it was established that the termitaries of *M. bellicosus* were always narrower in one plane than the other. A straight line through the widest diameter always pointed true east and west. In the neighbourhood of these last-mentioned termitaries, there was a palm tree 160 feet in height. Quite by chance, I found a covered-in termite runway going up the trunk, and vanishing into the foliage above. On investigation, we found that this passage was used by *Eutermes* workers for the purpose of fetching water from the top of the palm to their termitary, which was 60 feet from the foot of the tree.

I also took the opportunity to study the art of the *Eutermes* builders in more detail. While observing the building, I started to more fully contemplate the subject of nutrition. Claude Fuller and other observers call *Eutermes* the 'haymakers', and take it for granted that the grass collected by these termites is used for food. When a termitary belonging to *Eutermes* is examined, many passages filled with dry grass stalks of about half an inch in length are discovered. This grass is carried to the termitary at night, through passages that spread out in all directions. There are storerooms at intervals in these passages, where some of the grass is carefully stored. Even inside the termitary, there are sometimes parts filled to such an extent with grass that there is barely room for soldiers and workers to pass. This, according to the observers, is clearly their method of storing surplus food.

They arrived at this conclusion because there is such a large quantity stored, and so much of the termites' activity is centred on collecting it. There could have been no other basis for this conclusion on the observers' part, though no one has ever seen *Eutermes* eating grass, nor has anyone found grass within the body of the termite.

I actually abandoned this theory many years ago. I convinced myself, through microscopic examination, that *Eutermes* was not equipped for chewing grass and swallowing it; so I doubt very much whether the worker could do this. Its mouth parts are certainly more developed than those of the soldier are, but this development is directed towards specialised functions, such as the carrying of grains of sand, coating them with sticky fluid, the feeding of fluids to the queen and the larvae, and the severing of grass stalks. At the same time, they seem to be quite incapable of masticating and swallowing the latter.

Another reason which made me question the food theory was that I had never succeeded in finding under the microscope the least sign of grass in the entrails of either the workers or soldiers. All that I found was a fluid, which had every appearance of being derived from the moisture of the earth and the sap of plant roots.

Later, I learnt of research in South America which reinforced my conclusions. It is again worth recalling that the habits of ants and termites are often so much alike that the behaviour of one provides a key to the behaviour of the other.

In South America and Mexico, there is an ant known as the leaf-cutting ant. It does great damage to trees by cutting round pieces from the leaves. They drop these to the ground, where other workers are waiting to pounce on them and carry them to the nest. Without any further investigation, it was assumed that these leaves were used for food. However, an observer in Mexico proved that the leaves are never used for feeding purposes. Instead, they are packed in masses on the side of the nest where the heat of the sun is the most fierce. The theory of this observer is that the leaves serve the sole purpose of protection against the rays of the tropical sun. Whether this is the case is not definite, but it *is* definite that the leaves are not eaten, and do not serve as food.

I wondered whether *Eutermes* might be using grass for the same purpose. I soon realized, however, that this could not be the case, for the method of storing would not enable the grass to serve as protection against the sun.

All the architecture of *Eutermes* is based on the arch. They were probably the first 'architects' to discover the secret of arch building. It took many years of civilization before people discovered how to use the arch in architecture. Those extraordinary builders, the Egyptians, knew nothing of the arch and limited themselves to two vertical pillars with a colossal stone as a crossbeam. The Greeks and Romans did not understand the properties of the arch. It was only in the Middle Ages that architects came to understand fully the value of the arch in building.

It is very interesting to note that we find, in the architecture of the termite, two stages of development of the arch very similar to that used in our own architecture.

It is important to examine some building operations of the

Eutermes workers building an arch by gradual approximation of two pillars

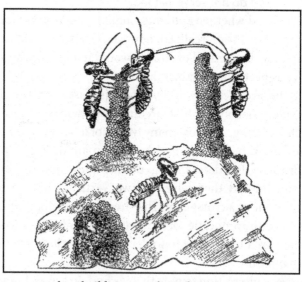

Eutermes workers building an arch. In this case a grass stalk is laid from pillar to pillar and is covered with tiny pebbles.

Eutermes after rain has fallen. One portion of the termitary has a dark stain. If this is examined with a magnifying glass, a wet patch will be found where the outer crust has disappeared. It is possible to cut away a small piece of this without causing enough disturbance to make the workers disappear.

The building of the first architects on earth can now be studied. It is clear that all the building of *Eutermes* is based on the arch. This arch is formed in two ways; the first, and most primitive, is made by inclining two vertical pillars towards each other until they meet. This is the way the first arch in our own society was created.

In the second and more involved method, every eighth worker or so carries in its mouth a grass-stalk instead of a pebble. The worker climbs up one of the pillars, quickly fastens one end of the stalk with sticky fluid to the top of the pillar, and then rushes away, without waiting to see what happens. The grass-stalk sinks slowly towards the other pillar, until its end comes to rest on the summit. We then see another worker waiting in readiness. As soon as the end of the stalk comes within its reach, the worker stretches up, grips it, and pulls it down to the summit of the pillar where in turn it is attached with fluid. On this crossbeam, the termites plaster tiny pebbles until a perfect arch is the result.

Success however, is not always assured. Occasionally the stalk remains vertical instead of sinking down. In these cases, the termites simply finish the arch by inclining the tops of the vertical pillars towards each other until they meet, while the stalk is eventually covered with masonry. Why the stalk is used at all, when the termites are able to finish the arch with pebbles only, is not possible to explain. Perhaps it is only a fundamental remainder of a principle which has disappeared. Whatever the explanation may be, I am positive *Eutermes* never uses the grass stalks as food.

15

The Queen in Her Cell

IT WAS NOT UNTIL LONG AFTER I had published most of my observations that I had, for the first time, an opportunity to investigate in more depth the most important phenomenon in the psychological life of the termite.

By this I mean the behaviour of the queen as a living and active part of the community. I had attempted hundreds of times on the *veld* to expose the palace cavity in such a manner that the functions of the queen and what occurs in her immediate vicinity would be visible to me. I had previously had the opportunity to watch the development of a nest, but my observations were cut short, and gave no insight into what happens later when the queen is sealed in her cell and continues life as the brain of the community.

An opportunity arose later in Pretoria. There was a house in Arloius Lane which had been infested with termites for years. They were continually causing great destruction and a number of attempts had been made in vain to rid the house of them. The queen had never been found and as soon as the damage to the house had been repaired, the termites' destruction started again. Finally, the Town Council undertook the work of exterminating them. Mr Victor Foster and I followed with great interest the labours of the workers while they were trying to track down the queen. After the searchers had tried in vain for many days to find the palace cavity, I made a suggestion to the supervisor.

I was convinced that in this case, there was only one queen, and that the community was not influenced by two or more queens, with the subjects swearing allegiance to another queen if their own were destroyed. I suggested that I would point out the palace cavity, on the condition that I might observe the living queen for two or three days. The supervisor agreed. Within a few minutes, I had identified three main passages and their point of intersection. I was then in a position to point out, with a fair degree of accuracy, the place where the queen's cell would be found. The palace cavity, luckily for us, was under a fireplace in the darkest corner of one of the rooms. Mr Foster and I exposed this ourselves, with the help of an electric torch. We succeeded in cutting, first the palace cavity, and then the actual cell of the queen in half, without causing undue disturbance to the community. We simply carved away a portion of the chamber wall and there before us lay the living, functioning brain of the organism. It was indeed a sight more wonderful than I had expected. I immediately regretted we had asked for only two or three days of observation.

Some of the phenomena which this exposure revealed to me I was acquainted with, and for these I watched. Others however, came as a complete surprise, and revealed amazing secrets.

This is what we saw. The queen was enormously big, and lay with her body pointing east and west, her head towards the west. The king, who of course was only the usual size of the flying termite, was constantly either on her gigantic body, or in its immediate neighbourhood. There was nothing in his behaviour that could in any way establish his function, although I made detailed notes on his every movement.

A large mass of the smaller class of worker was also in constant movement, both on the queen and around her. Immediately in front of the head of the queen was a small opening which served as an entrance and exit. This was, of course, far too small for the queen to pass through. Through

151

this small opening, two streams of workers were constantly passing, one coming in, and another going out. We very soon established that these small workers were occupied with three different tasks:

1) One stream was engaged in feeding the queen. Each worker stopped close to her head, and raised itself in order to reach her mouth. Immediately, a tiny drop of clear fluid appeared in its jaws, and would disappear at once into the mouth of the queen. As soon as the worker had given the fluid to the queen, the worker walked round her gigantic body, to reach the exit on the opposite side from that by which it had entered. The work continued with great speed and regularity, and none of the workers ever obstructed each other unnecessarily.

2) With these workers, and in the same streams, were some who had the task of carrying the eggs away and caring for them. These workers, too, walked right round the queen, to later appear carrying eggs in the outgoing stream. Mr Foster calculated that the queen laid 50,000 eggs in 24 hours, which gives some idea of the speed with which the task of conveying them had to be accomplished.

3) A much smaller group of workers was occupied with a far more perplexing task. I could not find out exactly what they were doing, but assumed they were busy cleaning the skin of the queen in some way. They were constantly engrossed, either singly or in groups, in some task on the queen's gigantic body. They appeared to be softly stroking her skin with their jaws in a continuous movement. We did discover that when they

entered the cell their bodies were empty, whereas when they left, they were filled with a colourless fluid. This fluid must, therefore, have been obtained in some way through the skin of the queen without in any way damaging it. We called these workers 'masseurs'.

It may be that they were appointed to some special work of feeding the young and that the queen secreted the fluid used for this purpose. I based this assumption on what we actually saw happening when we followed some of these masseurs after they had left the queen's cell. I still had some doubts about this observation, however, for we experienced some difficulty in keeping track of these workers.

It appeared, however, that the masseurs, after leaving the cell, visited one of the big breeding gardens, where there were a large number of the small white babies. Here, they fed the babies with drops of colourless fluid, in exactly the same way that other workers of this class fed the queen. It occurred to me therefore, that the body of the queen served as an organ for digesting food a stage further, for use by part of the community. A change occurs in her body which means that the nutriment is fit for infant feeding. If this is actually the case, it is the first appearance in nature of 'milk' secretion by the mother.

In addition to these three classes of workers and their never-ending activity, we observed an even more interesting phenomenon in the palace cavity. The cell of the queen was encircled by a ring of the bigger soldiers. These soldiers were equidistant from each other. The plane of the circle was at an angle of approximately 45 degrees. In the foreground of the palace cavity, the soldiers were standing on the floor, while at the opposite side, they were hanging upside down from the roof. All their heads were turned directly towards magnetic north.

This fact is of importance, because I am convinced that the magnetism of the earth has a noticeable effect on most kinds of termite, as has already been indicated in connection with the water-shaft in Africa and in the shape of the termitaries of the magnetic ant of Australia.

The members of this bodyguard, as it could be described, were, for most of the time, motionless. Every now and then, however, one of them became activated with a strange movement, a swaying to-and-fro of the head and foremost part of the body. This reminded me of the well-known termite dance described by observers. As soon as one member began these movements, within a few seconds the soldier to its right was infected, and the behaviour was in turn handed on to the next one. This continued, from one to another, until the peculiar dance had been transmitted right round the circle, to end where it had begun.

We also saw the changing of the guards. The new guards entered the palace cavity by a large opening nearly opposite the head end of the cell. They formed a second circle within the circle of the guards about to be relieved. The new guards gradually widened their circle to take their places between the old guards. This was the signal for the latter to leave the cell in single file by the same opening. This was the only activity we observed on the part of these soldiers.

What could be the function of this mysterious circle? Another observer, who later had the opportunity of seeing them in German West Africa, described them as real bodyguards, which fulfil the same function as royal bodyguards do in the case of a human king or queen. I, however, found it difficult to accept this theory. Any enemy which had succeeded in penetrating the nest this far would surely be capable of overcoming this single line of defence very easily. One must remember that such an enemy would have come through miles of passages where it would meet countless soldiers of the same class, who would withstand every inch of its approach with every possible means of attack and defence. If an enemy had succeeded in forcing its way this far, no mere circle of bodyguards would be of the slightest use. I was never successful in stirring up this bodyguard to attack. I could touch them with my finger and move them from side to side, without any of them making the least attempt to bite, something which any other soldier of the same class would have done immediately in any other part of the nest. They appeared to me to be semi-conscious, like chloroformed termites.

I formulated another theory. The termitary is such a perfect analogy to the physical body of an animal – with its brain, its stomach and liver, its bloodstream consisting of two kinds of corpuscles – that my inclination was to clarify any unknown phenomenon in the termite through comparison with the higher animals. *forcing the analogy*

It had always appeared that there was one similar organ lacking in the termitary. I had always felt that there should be some system with the function of linking up the community and its brain, the queen, such as is the case with the central nervous system of animals. I had always been searching for something which would be the functional equivalent of the *medulla oblongata* and the vertebral column; which would act as a link, carrying the mysterious influence of the queen to all parts of the community. It must be admitted that this is a theory that is supported by very few observations. Perhaps future researchers will have the opportunity to investigate this mysterious circle more thoroughly, and establish its functions. Of one thing we may be certain; such a complicated and regular phenomenon must have some definite purpose.

Another occurrence that took place during our observation also links closely to the theory of the organic unity of the termitary.

While we were watching, a fairly large piece of hard clay became detached from the edge of the roof of the cell and fell down heavily on the queen. Immediately, a series of extraordinary occurrences took place. The only effect that the shock had on the queen herself was that she began moving her head to-and-fro in a rhythmic manner. The workers immediately stopped all work within the cell and wandered round in aimless groups. The circle of bodyguards broke up at once and most of them vanished down the passages behind the palace cavity. Then we saw masses of tiny workers swarming into the palace cavity and cell. They swarmed over the queen in order to suck the fluid through her skin, in exactly the same way as the masseurs had done in normal circumstances. The king greedily took part in this draining of his mate. They succeeded so well, that within a few minutes, the skin of the queen was hanging in loose folds.

In the meantime, we visited far outlying parts of the nest, where the termites had been very active just before the accident. Even in the farthest parts, all work had ceased. The large soldiers and workers gathered in great excitement in different parts of the nest. There appeared to be a tendency to collect in groups. There was not the least doubt the shock to the queen was felt in the outermost parts of the termitary within a few minutes.

Recovery began in the same place where the first and greatest disturbance took place. Slowly, the workers stopped their assault on the queen. The bodyguards again took up their positions in a circle and the queen ceased the rhythmic movements of her head. She appeared to be recovering from the shock.

So quickly that it was barely possible to follow all the stages, normal activity began again. The only difference in conduct that I could notice was that the workers appeared to be speeding up the feeding of the queen, and before long, her body had resumed its usual gigantic size. The following day, all activity in the outermost parts of the termitary was again fully functioning.

*

That was the end of our observations. The council workers had occupied themselves with excavating and removing the breeding gardens in other rooms, but now the time given to us had ended.

The queen was removed from her cell and taken away captive; and after that, the activities and life of this nest ceased for good.

THE END

ALSO FROM OSIRAN

friend earthworm

friend
earthworm

THE PRACTICAL APPLICATION
OF A LIFETIME STUDY OF THE MOST
IMPORTANT ANIMAL IN THE WORLD

GEORGE OLIVER

by George Oliver

ISBN 978-0-9802976-1-4

172 pages

The problem facing civilization today is rebuilding the soil and restoring the earth to a form usable for food production. Through the slow processes of nature, it takes 500 to 1,000 years to lay down an inch of topsoil. Under favorable conditions, a task-force of earthworms can do the same job in five years.

The soil of the earth is in a terrible state, but steps can be taken to provide a hope for better farming, better crops, and better livestock. George Oliver spent over forty years studying the effect of earthworms on the soil.

These magnificent creatures have been with us since the dawn of time, and the impact they have on all life is truly astounding. Whether you are interested in agriculture, poultry farming or fishing, this book is an excellent resource.

Drawing on a lifetime of study, Dr. Oliver does a commendable job of backing up all his information with thoroughly researched facts and figures.

This classic text, first published in 1941, has been re-edited for the modern reader.

Contents: History of the Earthworm / The Habits of the Earthworm / Habits of the Newly Developed Earthworm / Potential Markets for Earthworms / What is Food? / The Life Germ and Better Poultry / Economical Poultry Housing / The Interior of the Economical Hennery / Intensive Range / Putting the Bluebottle Fly to Work / Natural and Man-made Enemies of the Earthworm / The Trout Farmer's Problem / Feeding Problem of the Frog Farmer / Housing the Earthworm Stock / General Care and Feeding of Earthworms

Appendices: My Grandfather's Earthworm Farm / Introduction to Harvesting the Earthworm / On Earthworms

Béchamp or Pasteur?

A Lost Chapter in the History of Biology

by Ethel D. Hume

352 pages
ISBN 978-0980297607

This volume contains new editions of two titles which have been available only sporadically in the decades since their publication.

R. Pearson's *Pasteur: Plagiarist, Imposter* was originally published in 1942, and is a succinct introduction to both Louis Pasteur and Antoine Bechamp, and the reasons behind the troubled relationship that they shared for their entire working lives.

Whereas Pearson's work is a valuable introduction to an often complex topic, it is Ethel Douglas Hume's expansive and well-documented *Bechamp or Pasteur? A Lost Chapter in the History of Biology* which provides the main body of evidence. It covers the main points of contention between Bechamp and Pasteur in depth sufficient to satisfy any degree of scientific or historical scrutiny, and it contains, wherever possible, detailed references to the source material and supporting evidence.

Virtually no claim in Ms Hume's book is undocumented. The reader will soon discern that neither Mr Pearson nor Ms Hume could ever be called fans of Pasteur or his 'science'. They both declare their intentions openly; that they wish to contribute to the undoing of a massive medical and scientific fraud.

The text of both titles has been extensively re-edited so as to modernise the use of English, and make the book easier to read than has been the case with previous facsimile editions. Included are new renderings of all the diagrams that were included in the original edition of *Pasteur: Plagiarist, Imposter*, plus there is a small collection of what photographs of Professor Bechamp are available.

Ten Acres is Enough

by Edmund Morris

ISBN: 978-0980297638

214 pages

"Recently we have seen a great back-to-the-land movement, with many young professional people returning to small scale farming; thus it is great fun to read about someone who did exactly the same thing in 1864. In that year, Mr. Edmund Morris gave up his business and city life for a farm of ten acres, made a go of mixed farming and then wrote a book about it. Mr. Morris proves Abraham Lincoln's prediction: 'The greatest fine art of the future will be the making of a comfortable living from a small piece of land.'

Kudos to *Osiran Books* for resurrecting this fascinating treasure."
– *Sally Fallon Morell, President, The Weston A. Price Foundation*

This book has something for everyone; for the small farmer, the home gardener, the city dweller who wonders whether there might not be a better life in the country — and for anyone who has an idea, and needs just a spark of courage and inspiration to make it happen. This book may be about farming and homesteading, and indeed it is a delightfully readable autobiography of a farmer in the America of the 1860s, but it also about much, much more. The challenges that faced the author are timeless, as are his courage, commitment, and ingenuity. There are insights for anyone, farmer or not, in this book.

Tꓭꓢ Wꓧꓰꓰꓡ Oꜰ HꓰꓯꓡTꓧ

by Guy Wrench

ISBN: 978-0-9802976-6-9
182 pages

Good health is an attractive state, but it can be a very dull topic. Everything depends on how it is approached. Dr Wrench attracts our attention at once, by asking "Why not research health as well as disease?"

To him it is more interesting to know why we are not as healthy as we should be, than it is to ask why we are as diseased as we are. Naturally he had difficulty in finding people in whom he could study health as a natural characteristic, but finally found what he wanted in the small tribe of the Hunza in Northern Pakistan. The very place itself has its fascination, lying hidden high up in one of the tremendous clefts amongst the 'congress of great mountains' separating Pakistan from China and Russia.

The Hunza are people of extraordinary physique and health, and this is largely attributed by Dr Wrench to the fact that their foods, such as vegetables and wheat, are not 'sophisticated', as Robert McCarrison calls it, by the artificial processes applied by Westerners. How these processes affect our food is dealt with in great detail. The argument is detailed and is attractively presented. Whether there is much likelihood of Dr Wrench's views being widely adopted is open to question, but they are impressive. The simplicity of Hunza life is greatly to be desired. Our western civilization will never adopt it *in toto*, but we could take some elements of it to heart.

This book will appeal to all who interest themselves in health and the principles of its maintenance.